GEMLORE

Borgo Press Books by Michael R. Collings

All Calm, All Bright: Christmas Offerings
Brian Aldiss
Dark Transformations: Deadly Visions of Change
The Films of Stephen King
GemLore: An Introduction to Precious and Semi-Precious Gem-
  stones
The House Beyond the Hill: A Novel of Horror
The Many Facets of Stephen King
Naked to the Sun: Dark Visions of Apocalypse
Piers Anthony
Scaring Us to Death: The Impact of Stephen King on Popular Cul-
  ture
Singer of Lies: A Novel of Fantasy
Wordsmith, Part One: The Veil of Heaven: A Science Fantasy Novel
Wordsmith, Part Two: The Thousand Eyes of Flame: A Science Fan-
  tasy Novel

GEMLORE

AN INTRODUCTION TO PRECIOUS AND SEMI-PRECIOUS STONES

Second Edition, Revised and Enlarged

by

Michael R. Collings

Emeritus Professor of English
Seaver College
Pepperdine University

THE BORGO PRESS

An Imprint of Wildside Press LLC

MMIX

Borgo Reference Guides
ISSN 0891-9607

Number Two

www.wildsidepress.com

SECOND EDITION

In all civilizations, magical powers have been ascribed to gems—perhaps out of a need to explain their rarity, beauty, and strangeness in a confusing world. Color played a great role in the symbolism: gold for the sun; blue for the sky, heaven, or sea; red for blood; black for death. Colors were also associated with the planets and astrology—gems became connected here as well. Durability was also important—the unsurpassed hardness of diamond reflects in the belief that it will bring its wearer strength and invincibility. (Sofianides and Harlow 20).

in all prehistoric magical powers have these attributes
[unclear faded text] perhaps which a prime [unclear] that many beautiful
and courageous and majestic [unclear] Color named a great
role in every [unclear] and for the artist this is the
best known and [unclear] black for many colors were
also produced with red black and and blue [unclear] of
plants produced dye as well. Durability was the [unclear]
and that inspired head and the common objects being
left bright with which [unclear] work although any responsibility.
(Schneider and below [?])

GEMLORE

BIRTHSTONES

The tradition of birthstones dates back to about the first century A.D. and relates to the twelve stones that adorned the High Priest's Breastplate in the Old Testament. The contemporary traditions of birthstones began during the eighteenth century in Poland and from there spread throughout the world.

Different cultures associated various stones with the months. Among the most accepted pairings today are the following:

January	Garnet
February	Amethyst
March	Aquamarine
April	Diamond
May	Emerald
June	Pearl
July	Ruby
August	Peridot
September	Sapphire
October	Opal
November	Golden Topaz/Citrine
December	Blue Topaz

[A somewhat more cynical viewpoint might make the connection between the commercial appeal of birthstones and the fact that the more expensive gemstones appear in most lists.]

WIND AND STONE

I am stone
enclosed by wind.

We share damp shores.
We hear black waves break
on charcoal knots
that stud bleak shells
of rotted logs.

We breathe the breath
of pines that sway
urgent needles
sunward, earthward—
elegant arcs
ride surrounding winds.

We taste the trail
of water on air.
We smell and taste
and touch—river
and cove ripe
with wild strawberry.

You lean into the wind,
stroke its smoothness
into glass, release,
evaporate,
and supple-shape again.
You are wind.

You touch and warm
and move with subtlety
into thin crevices,
too thin to see.
You penetrate
dark hollow hearts

of stone

LEGEND:

❖ Historical and cultural information about the minerals and rocks

➢ Names for each mineral or rock and their meanings

• Properties attributed to or associated with each mineral or rock in various historical and/or contemporary traditions, including purported healing and mind-enhancing powers, mystical (and non-verifiable) lore, and folklore

[Given the variety of interpretations and beliefs possible, *Gemlore* lists some of the more interesting but makes no attempt to be either definitive or inclusive.]

GEMLORE

— A —

ABALONE, MOTHER-OF-PEARL, PAUA SHELL

❖ Not a gemstone per se, but a organic, nacreous, pearly material found on the interior of the shell of a large mollusk (also called *abalone*)

➢ *Abalone*: American Spanish, *abulon*, from Costanoan (California coastal Indian dialect), *aluuan* 'red abalone'

• Calms, alleviates fears

ACTINOLITE

❖ One variety of actinolite is nephrite, or JADE

❖ A second gemstone variety is cat's-eye actinolite, which shows a distinct *chatoyancy*, similar to that of TIGER'S EYE QUARTZ

➢ *Actinolite*: Greek, *aktin* 'ray' + *lite* 'rock or part of a rock'; so named because it frequently occurs in long needle-like crystals or 'rays'

➢ *Actinolated Quartz*: Included as long grass-green to black needle-like crystals in transparent QUARTZ

- Associated with Scorpio
- Associated with the number 4
- Brings the wearer joy, luck, and wisdom (although to a lesser degree than jade)
- Promotes brotherhood (and, presumably, sisterhood)
- Allows the wearer to overcome unwanted conditions
- Soothes the wearer
- Strengthens the needs and awareness of the body
- Generally has the same healing properties as Jade

ADULARIA [SEE MOONSTONE]

AGATE

See also CHALCEDONY, CARNELIAN, CHRYSOPRASE, MOSS AGATE

- ❖ Earliest appearances: Stone Age cultures in France, circa 20,000 B.C.
- ❖ Sumerians and Babylonians: Agate axe heads dating some 5,000 years ago
- ❖ Egyptians: As ornaments before 3,000 B.C.
- ❖ Birthstone for Taurus, the Bull
- ❖ Traditional gemstone for the 12th Anniversary
- ❖ *Moss Agate*: Gemstone for the 14th Anniversary
- ❖ Much Brazilian agate is naturally gray but subsequently dyed using a variety of minerals and treatments to create vivid colors and markings:
    Red: Iron oxide
    Yellow: Iron chloride
    Brown: Sugar solution and heat
    Black: Carbon
    Green: Iron
    Blue, Berliner blue: Iron
- ❖ Authorities list nearly 3,000 names for agate varieties

❖ *Agate*: One of two state gemstones of Montana

❖ *Blue Agate*: State gem of Nebraska

❖ *Fairburn Agate, Fairburnite*: State gemstone of South Dakota

❖ *Lake Superior, Duluth, Keweenaw or Royale Agate*: State gemstone of Minnesota

❖ *Prairie Agate*: State rock of Nebraska

➢ *Agate*: Named for the Achates (*Akhates*) River in Sicily

➢ *Agate:* Alternate etymology, from Greek *agateec* 'happy'

➢ *Blue Lace Agate*: Delicate sky-blue and white layers, often suggesting scallops

➢ *Botswana Agate*: From *Botswana*, Africa; grey, black, pink, and cream layers

➢ *Brecciated Agate*: Agate layers fractured but held together by naturally formed QUARTZ cement

➢ *Dendritic Agate, Mocha Stone:* Misnomer for a non-layered CHALCEDONY variety; shows dainty fern-like internal structures formed from manganese and other mineral inclusions

➢ *Cloud Agate*: Grey with blurry or foggy patches

➢ *Enhydrous Agate, Enhydritic Agate*: Nodule containing water-filled bubbles, seen from the outside when held to the light

➢ *Eye Agate*: Variety of orbicular agate, concentric rings of agate layers around a central point

➢ *Fairburn Agate*: Named for *Fairburn*, South Dakota; a particularly fine variety of fortification agate

➢ *Fire Agate:* Displays an opal-like play of colors, caused by included GOETHITE or limonite, often suggesting internal bubbles or nodules

➢ *Fortification Agate*: Agate layers form jutting corners, suggesting the battlements of a fort

➢ *Iris Agate*: Iridescent variety, particularly color-filled when cut as thin slabs

➢ *Mexican Lace Agate or Crazy-Lace Agate:* Characterized by rich, deep colors in complex bands

➢ *Mosquito Stone, Midge Stone*: Dendritic agate in which the dendrites do not cluster in masses but rather appear in small ball-like growths

➤ *Nipomo Agate*: Named for *Nopomo,* California; Included with MARCASITE
➤ *Orbicular Agate*: Circles of layered agate around a central point
➤ *Petoskey Stone*: Agatized fresh-water CORAL
➤ *Plume Agate*: Inclusions form plume-like or feather-like patterns
➤ *Polka Dot Agate*: Contains yellow, polka-dot-like inclusions
➤ *Rainbow Agate*: Sliced slabs exhibit a spectrum of colors
➤ *Scenic Agate*: Misnomer for a non-layered CHALCEDONY in which dendritic inclusions suggest landscapes
➤ *Snakeskin Agate*: Named for the snake-like outer surface of un-cut rough; red-brown with black bands
➤ *Star Agate*: Variety occasionally displaying ray-like bands
➤ *Thunder Egg, Donnerei* (German, 'thunder egg'): Layered nod-ule with heavily textured outer surface and agate interior
➤ *Tubular Agate*: Contains remnants of tubes, originally feeding canals, surrounded by agate layers
➤ *Turritella Agate, Turntell Agate*: Includes small fossilized shells

• Associated with Fire, Water (particularly *Moss Agate*); the planet Mercury; Gemini and Taurus; and the number 7
• Ancients: Agate makes the wearer invisible
• Hindus: Enables children to overcome fears, learn to walk, and develop balance
• Persians: Used magically to divert storms
• Greeks and Romans: Agate brought protection and instilled courage; particularly potent when worn in battle
• Native American and Mexican cultures: Fire Agate encourages regeneration and energizes the spirit
• Placed in cooking utensils and drinking water to insure health and ward off illness
• Believed to cure scorpion stings and snake bites.
• Believed to calm thunder and lightning

- 11th Century: Enhances the wearer's powers of persuasion
- 14th Century: Averts lightning and storms
- Set in gold—alleviates symptoms of slow metabolism
- Placed in water—ameliorates illness
- Stabilizing stone, calming to a troubled mind
- Ideal as a "worry stone" or "worry bead"
- Counter the negative effect (to its wearer) of stone's worn by other persons
- Promotes fidelity in marriage
- *Blue Lace Agate*: Enhances grace and lightheartedness; associated with Pisces
- *Botswana Agate*: Traditionally enhances attentiveness to detail; associated with Scorpio and the number 3
- *Crazy Lace Agate:* Placed under the pillow, cures insomnia and brings pleasant dreams
- *Fire Agate*: Burns excess energies; associated with Aries and the number 9
- *Green Agate:* Traditionally enhances forthrightness and decisiveness
- *Iris Agate*: Associated with Sagittarius and the number 44
- *Mexican Crazy-Lace Agate*: Associated with Aries and the number 7
- *Polka Dot Agate*: Associated with Gemini and the number 2
- *Snakeskin Agate*: Associated with Scorpio and the number 2

ICESTORM

At Christmas, IceStorm lightning does not
    Streak
    Or shriek
Stark jagged jets across pitch sky
Through thunderheads that lie

Like shaggy bundles piled on an agate
>Sheet—
>With heat
And violence to twist the night
And put calm dreams to flight.

No, lightning does not burn at Christmas-time,
>Burn
>Or churn
Or wrench awry …. In honor of
The Infant Child of Love

The lightning does not slice in zagging cuts but
>Swirls
>Encurls
Encloses snow-draped vales and crests
With silver-gleaming, silver-sheening rest.

ALABASTER, SATIN SPAR

❖ Fine-grained, translucent variety of GYPSUM, soft enough to be carved and polished by hand; also a variety of CALCITE
❖ Carved artifacts 6,000 years old have been found in modern Syria
❖ Used by all early Mediterranean cultures for sculpting and carving
❖ Particularly valued by the Etruscans who, among other uses, carved alabaster sarcophagi
❖ Used by ancient Egyptians to carve canopic jars to hold the viscera removed from bodies prior to mummification
❖ Cut in thin sheets, translucent enough to serve in windows

➢ *Alabaster*: Greek, *alabastros, alabastos*, possibly derived from Egyptian city of *Alabastron*; alternatively, Egyptian, *alabastrites*, 'stone from which alabastron vases were made'
➢ *Florentine Marble*: Name applied to vases and figures carved of Italian alabaster
➢ *Mexican Onyx*: Misnomer for alabaster (calcite variety) from Mexico exported to the United States
➢ *Oriental Alabaster*: Banded CALCITE, frequently the "alabaster" referred to by ancient cultures

ALEXANDRITE [SEE CHRYSOBERYL]

AMAZONITE, AMAZON STONE

- ❖ Rich blue or green variety of FELDSPAR
- ❖ Hebrews: The third stone in the breastplate worn by the High Priests in the Old testament
- ❖ Pike's Peak, Colorado, is the world's most important source of amazonite; other deposits occur elsewhere in Colorado and in the Ilmen Mountains of Russia
- ❖ Contemporary alternate birthstone for December

- ➢ *Amazonite*: *Amazon* + *ite* 'rock or part of a rock'
- ➢ Though the name derives from the Amazon River basin, no deposits have been found there

- • Associated with Virgo and the number 5
- • Ancient Egyptians: Amulets of amazonite contained strong magic
- • Improves the skin
- • Releases fear and anxiety
- • Used as an elixir, helpa balance the body's calcium needs

AMBER

- ❖ One of the few organic gemstones (along with CORAL, IVORY, JET, and PEARL)
- ❖ True amber must be several millions of years old, generally ranging from 30 to 90 million years; more recently fossilized or hardened resin is called COPAL, or young amber
- ❖ The most important source of amber is the Baltic coast; other deposits occur in Sicily, England, Burma, the Dominican Republic, Mexico, and New Jersey
- ❖ All species of trees that originally produced amber—including primarily cedars and other conifers—are now extinct
- ❖ Amber containing fossilized insects, spiders, and other organic material is often most highly prized; as shown in the movie *Jurrasic Park,* such amber may include remnant DNA of long-

extinct species

❖ Fashioned into amulets and beads by ancient cultures as long as 10,000 years ago

➢ Arabic: *Ambar* 'ambergris'—a substance found in whales and used in making perfumes

➢ Greek: *Elektron,* associated with the sun (hence the root of such modern words as *electric* and *electron*); when rubbed, AMBER produces an electrostatic charge

➢ German: *Bernstein* [*brennen* 'burn'] 'burn-stone'—when heated, AMBER will soften and eventually burn

➢ *Baltic Amber*: Found along the *Baltic* Sea near Kaliningrad (formerly Königsberg), Russia, the source of nearly 90% of the world's amber; generally considered the finest variety

➢ *Burmite*: Amber from Burma; deeper red, harder, and denser than Baltic amber

➢ *Simetite*: Named for a Sicilian river along which it is found

• Associated with Fire; Sun and Leo; Mercury; and the number 3

• Associated with tears of the gods, tears of the sun, and tears of trees

• Anciently: Worn by babies, would help in teething

• Greek mythology: Amber formed when Phaeton, son of the sun-god Helios, was killed. His grieving sisters were transformed into poplar trees, and their tears became amber

• Demonstratus, 1st Century Roman historian: Referred to amber as *lyncurius,* solidified lynx urine, differentiating male and female urin by color

• Provides focus for renewed wedding vows; seals oaths and protects warriors

• Increases vitality, motivation, and creativity

• Attracts loyal friends into the wearer's life

• Absorbs negative energy and transforms it into positive

• Enhances the wearer's beauty

AMBLYGONITE

❖ Transparent crystals faceted for gemstones, although it is relatively soft and breakable

❖ Locations include Saxony; France; Maine; Pala, California; and Black Hills, South Dakota

➤ *Amblygonite*: Greek, *amblus* 'blunt' + Greek, *gouia* 'angle' + *ite* 'rock or mineral', named for the shape of its crystal

➤ *Montebrasite*: Variety from Montebras, Creuse, France

➤ *Hebronite*: Variety from Hebron, Maine

AMETHYST

❖ Deep purple to lilac variety of QUARTZ

❖ Early references: Egyptians formed amulets in the form of animals, circa 3,000 B.C.

❖ Requires irradiation, either natural or artificial, to gain its deep color; direct sunlight may cause some amethyst varieties to fade

❖ Among the most highly valued semi-precious gemstones; at one time, included with DIAMOND, SAPPHIRE, RUBY, and EMERALD as a cardinal (or most valuable) gemstone

❖ When heated, amethyst turns yellow; most CITRINE is probably heat-treated amethyst

❖ At 7 on the Mohs scale, amethyst is among the hardest semi-precious gemstones; even so, it is only about 1/15 the hardness of DIAMOND

❖ Huge AGATE GEODES found in Brazil and elsewhere are often lined with amethyst and are called amethyst cathedrals.

❖ Amethyst banded with CITRINE is called AMETRINE

❖ Traditional birthstone for February

❖ Traditional gemstone for Wednesday

➤ *Amethyst*: Greek, *amethustos* 'anti-intoxicant' [from: *a* 'not' + *methuskein* 'to intoxicate']

➤ Greek Mythology: Angered by an insult, the God Bacchus vowed to destroy the next person he saw, which happened to be the nymph Amethyst, or Amethystos, a follower of Diana. As Bacchus's tigers sprang to devour the nymph, Diana transformed her into a clear crystal. Later, sorrowing for the result of his anger, Bacchus poured a libation of wine over the stone, coloring it purple.

➢ Greek Mythology: While drunk, Dionysus pursued the nymph Amethystos, who prayed to Artemis to preserve her chastity. Artemis transformed her into a pillar of pure crystal, later stained purple when Dionysus poured an offering of wine over it in tribute to her chastity.

- Associated with Pisces, Aries, Aquarius, Capricorn, and Sagittarius; with the planets Jupiter and Neptune; with Water; and with the number 3
- Greeks: Prevents intoxication—drinking vessels made from amethyst crystals might contain clear water, yet the drinker would appear to be consuming red wine
- Rome: Amethyst pendant tied with a dog's hair cord cures snake bite
- Hebrews: Stimulates dreams and visions
- Medieval Europe: As an amulet, protects its wearer from harm in battle
- 16th Century Europe: Enhances shrewdness and business sense
- Provides protection from storms at sea and from drowning
- Carries a powerful healing influence
- Calms anger and relieves unbridled passions
- Brings prophetic dreams and visions
- Alleviates insomnia
- Prevents oversleeping
- Facilitates a sense of peace and balance

ANNIVERSARY

Anniversary—
    Gold-wire butterfly ring
      With amethyst wings

Iris blooms above
Earth drowsing in glimmer-dew—
Dreams of Amethyst

AMETHYSTINE CHALCEDONY [SEE DAMSONITE]

AMETRINE, TRYSTINE, BOLIVIANITE [TRADE NAME]

❖ Naturally occurring variety of quartz with mixed zones of amethyst and citrine
❖ Almost all Ametrine mined in Bolivia, with some deposits in Brazil and India
❖ The color gradient reflect different oxidation of iron in the crystal
❖ Artificial Ametrine created by controlled heating of AMETHYST-crystals

➤ *Ametrine*: Named for its constituent minerals, AME-thyst and ci-TRINE

AMMOLITE [SEE ARAGONITE]

ANDALUSITE [SEE CHASTOLITE]

❖ Faceted when found in gem-quality, transparent, greenish or reddish square crystals
❖ The finest gem-quality specimens occur as water-rounded pebbles

➤ *Andalusite*: Named for *Andalusia,* the Spanish province where it was first found + *ite* 'rock or mineral'

ANGLESITE

❖ Pale green, blue, yellow, white, and colorless mineral, essentially oxidized GALENA

- ❖ Classified as a gemstone, but quite fragile
- ❖ Faceted only as collectors' specimens
- ❖ Tumbled massive specimens (non-crystalline) occasionally wire-wrapped

- ➢ *Anglesite*: Named after *Anglesey*, an island in Wales, where it was first discovered + *ite* 'rock or mineral'

- • Associated with Pisces and the number 2
- • Useful in channeling and communicating with spirits
- • Grounding stone

APACHE TEARS

- ❖ Small rounded nodules of black to grey OBSIDIAN, often found in a grey-white matrix of perlite, amorphous volcanic glass

- ➢ The name stems from a legend about the Apache tribe. Following a surprise attack by the U.S. military in retaliation for an earlier Apache raid, the few survivors leaped over a cliff to avoid being killed or captured. The Apache Tears are the tears shed for them by their wives and children.

APATITE

- ❖ Among the lesser minerals as gemstones, apatite is a primary source of the essential mineral phosphorus, necessary for all living organisms—occasionally, however, crystals do appear as gems
- ❖ Fine-grained massive apatite a major constituent in bones and teeth
- ❖ Cabochon-cut gemstone-quality blue cat's-eye apatite occasionally available, generally from Burma and Sri Lanka
- ❖ Crystals occasionally large enough for faceting, although the mineral is quite brittle and generally confined to collectors
- ❖ Crystals range from colorless to yellow, green, blue, and violet
- ❖ One crystal in the Smithsonian Institution in Washington D.C. weighs 500 carats

> *Apatite*: Greek, *apatos* 'deception—I am misleading,' + *ite* 'mineral or rock'; so named because its wide range of shapes and colors frequently leads to confusion with other minerals.
> *Asparagus Stone*: Deep yellow-green crystals from Spain, so named for their color

- Associated with Fire, Air, and Earth
- Characterized by its electromagnetic energy
- Exerts an emotionally calming effect, especially during times of stress

APOPHYLLITE
❖ Associated with Libra and Gemini
❖ Few uses other than as collectors' minerals, popular for their well-defined, beautiful crystals
❖ Most readily accessible samples come from Poona, India

> *Apophyllite*: Greek *apo* 'off' + *phyl-* 'leaf'; *apophylliso* 'it flakes off'; crystals tend to flake off when heated

- Enables one to distinguish between truth and falsehood
- Associated with magnetic energy flow
- Facilitates mental clarity and insight

AQUAMARINE
❖ Blue variety of BERYL
❖ Earliest recorded sources: Greeks, between 480 and 300 B.C.
❖ Popular as a gemstone since the 17th Century
❖ Aquamarine differs from EMERALD primarily in color
❖ Among the hardest gemstones, with a Mohs hardness of 7.5-8.0, exceeded only by CORUNDUM (RUBY) and DIAMOND
❖ The largest mined, discovered in 1910 in Brazil, weighed over 100 kg, and was 48.5 cm long and 42 cm in diameter
❖ One crystal, weighing over 200 pounds, discovered in Brazil; sent to Germany, where it was cut into 200,000 carats of smaller stones
❖ Gemstone for Pisces along with BLOODSTONE; and for Gemini

- ❖ Traditional birthstone for March
- ❖ Gemstone for 16th and 19th Wedding Anniversaries

- ➤ *Aquamarine*: Latin *aqua* 'water' + *mare* 'sea'

- • Associated with Gemini, Pisces, and Aries; the Moon; Water; and the number 1
- • Romans: Amulets protected sailors from enemies at sea, especially when inscribed with figures of Poseidon and his chariot
- • Early Christians: Symbolized happiness and eternal youth
- • Associated with water-divination
- • Stone of tranquility, able to bring the wearer calmness
- • Cooling effects aid in breaking fevers
- • Cures motion sickness
- • Symbol of happiness and eternal youth
- • Stone of courage

ARAGONITE
- ❖ Chemically identical to CALCITE but with a differing crystallization pattern
- ❖ Known as a separate mineral as early as 1797
- ❖ Occurs in white, yellow, or pink crystals or aggregates
- ❖ Clusters of outwardly radiating, six-sided crystals popular as collectors' specimens
- ❖ Associated with MOTHER-OF-PEARL formed in the shells of some mollusks
- ❖ Forms the iridescent material in the shells of extinct ammonites, also called AMMOLITE

- ➤ *Aragonite*: Named after *Aragon*, where it was first found + *ite* 'rock or mineral'

ARAZONITE [SEE DAMSONITE]

ASTORITE
- ❖ Unique material from the Astor (or Toltec) Mine in southwestern Colorado

- ❖ Mine named for John Jacob Astor IV (once considered the wealthiest man in America), the previous owner, who died aboard the *Titanic* in 1912; the entrance was sealed after his death and not re-opened until 2001
- ❖ Mine the sole source of an amalgam of RHODONITE, RHODO-CHROSITE, and QUARTZ, streaked with flecks, grains, and tiny fibers of SILVER, GOLD, COPPER, LEAD, and chalcopyrite
- ❖ Pink, red, clear, white, and dark granular material takes a high polish and works well when cut *en cabochon* or as freeforms
- ❖ Cut slices show an attractive play of light and reflections even without polishing

- ➢ *Astorite*: From John Jacob *Astor* IV + *ite* 'rock or mineral'

AVENTURINE QUARTZ
- ❖ QUARTZ colored by inclusions of chromium mica or HEMATITE flakes
- ❖ Occurs in a range of colors—including green, orange, peach, brown, and gray—but the green variety provides the most common gemstones
- ❖ The main modern source is India
- ❖ *Green Aventurine*: Contemporary birthstone for August
- ❖ Gemstone for 8th wedding anniversary

- ➢ *Aventurine*: Italian, *a ventura* 'by chance'—the gemstone received its name from a Renaissance glass of a similar color; artisans in Venetian glass claimed that even if one followed the formula for that particular gold-flecked glass, the results more often were determined by chance [*a ventura*] rather than by art. "Goldstone" is the generally accepted name for the contemporary version of *Aventurine* glass.
- ➢ The glittering effect of the mica-inclusions is called *aventurescence*

- • Associated with Aries and the number 3
- • Traditionally enhances leadership
- • A 'Nature' stone, attracting peace, serenity, and tranquility; abundance and prosperity

- Releases fear and anxiety
- Increases confidence and gratitude
- Useful in good luck spells
- Shields the heart

AVENTURINE DRAGONFLY

Spring-fly   wing-fly-flitting
splitting light from shadow
swallow draft-draught of somnolence
caught moss-to-moss   Immobile
gold-glint greening-preening-sheening
iridesced translucency—
weed-reed bower-building boulder-welding
knot-knitter   moonstone-pebble-rubble
crafting into art
               weaving bare-air
patterns spring to torpid summer

AXINITE

- ❖ Brown to violet-brown or reddish-brown axe-shaped crystals
- ❖ Considered a gemstone but its value is limited by the small size of crystals, rarely more than 5 carats (.035 oz.) and the fact that most are heavily flawed
- ❖ Relatively large crystals from Crestmore, California, however, are faceted as collectors' specimens
- ❖ Long considered a brown variety of TOURMALINE, established as a separate mineral in the early 1800s

- ➤ *Axinite*: From Greek, *axin* 'axe' + *ite* 'rock or mineral'

AZURITE, CHESSYLITE

- ❖ Anciently crushed and used as a blue pigment, *Azurro della Magna* [Ironically, even though it provided one of the most expensive coloring agents, azurite proved less durable than painters anticipated. Over the centuries, many of the azurite-based blues continued their natural and inexorable chemical transformation into malachite—with the often unsettling effect of giving those areas originally painted blue a deep greenish cast.]

❖ Frequently found in conjunction with MALACHITE and CHRYSOCOLLA; all are copper derivatives

❖ Since it is relatively soft, azurite is less frequently used in jewelry, usually appearing a cabochons

❖ Occasionally faceted, but crystals are generally too soft, too dark, and too opaque to be effective

❖ Since azurite naturally weathers into MALACHITE, collectors frequently store outstanding samples in cool, dark, sealed environments to retard its loss of brilliance

➢ *Azurite*: Old French, *azur* 'blue' + *ite* 'rock or part of a rock'

➢ *Azure*: Persian, *Lazhward,* an area renowned for deposits of *Lapis Lazuli*

➢ *Burnite*: Azurite intergrown with cuprite

➢ *Chessylite*: Alternate name from *Chessy,* near Lyons in France + *lite* 'rock or mineral'

• Associated with Water; Jupiter and Pisces; Moon; Venus

• Also associated with Sagittarius and the number 1

• Mentioned anciently in Pliny the Elder's *Natural History*

• Referred to as the "Stone of Heaven"

• Aids spiritual strengths and abilities

• Promotes flexibility in thought and action

• Enables the wearer to overcome obstacles

• Worn next to the skin, azurite stimulates empathy, compassion, love

• Alleviates symptoms of anxiety attacks, panic, anorexia and bulimia

• Deep blue specimens help develop psychic abilities through the third eye (pituitary center)

— B —

BARITE, BARYTES, HEAVY SPAR
- ❖ Chief source of barium, used in gastroenterological X-rays and in making fireworks

- ➤ *Barite*: Greek *barutes*, from *barus* 'heavy'

- • Associated with Earth and Fire; Venus and Taurus; Sun and Leo; Mars and Scorpio
- • Also associated with Aquarius and the number 1
- • Enables its wearer to believe that all things are possible
- • Facilitates clearing obstacles from the wearer's path
- • Alleviates depression—may induce laughter if held in the hand long enough

BENITOITE
- ❖ Extremely rare; found almost exclusively in the United States
- ❖ Official state gemstone of California
- ❖ Crystals initially mistaken for SAPPHIRES
- ❖ Dichroic; shows SAPPHIRE blue when viewed from one direction, colorless when viewed from another
- ❖ "Fire" almost as brilliant as that of DIAMOND, although frequently muted by the deep blue color
- ❖ Largest crystals may reach more than 2 inches in diameter
- ❖ Faceted primarily for collectors; colorless crystals generally not faceted

- ➤ *Benitoite*: Named for San *Benito* County, California, where it was discovered in 1906 + *ite* 'rock or mineral'

BERTRANDITE
- ❖ Bertrandite, closely related to BERYL, is a major source of beryl-

lium, a particularly important material for aerospace and nuclear technologies and COPPER alloys

❖ In crystal form colorless or pale yellow; dendritic bertrandite forms a deep purple stone, mottled with white and black

❖ The primary source for bertrandite was a single mine in southern Utah, now closed to collecting, where the stone was crushed for its beryllium content; only in recent years has the stone become considered a semi-precious stone

❖ With CHAROITE, bertrandite ranks among the most sought-after naturally purple semi-precious gemstones

➢ *Bertrandite*; Named for Leon *Bertrand*, a French mineralogist + *ite* 'rock or mineral'

➢ Also referred to as *Tiffany Stone, Tiffany Opal, Opalite, Ice Cream Opal, Opalized Fluorite, Bertrandite AGATE*, and "*Purple Passion*"

BERYL

❖ Beryl can form huge crystals; one of the largest is some 60 feet long and weighs 36 tons

❖ Massive, non-crystalline beryl is a major source of BERYLLIUM

❖ German word for 'eyeglasses', *Brille*, derived from *beryl*, since early lenses were ground from its crystals

❖ Traditional gemstone for Pisces

➢ *Beryl*: Greek, *berullos*, probably the name of the Southern Indian city of *Velur [Belur]*

➢ *Aquamarine*: Blue variety

➢ *Bixbite*: Extremely rare red variety, not suitably for jewelry since the crystals are almost always small

➢ *Emerald*: Green variety; most valued as a gemstone

➢ *Golden beryl*: Bright yellow variety; among the less valuable of precious beryl varieties

➢ *Goshenite*: Colorless, transparent variety

➢ *Heliodor*: Yellow variety

➢ *Morganite*: Pink variety; strongly colored and much in demand

- Associated with Fire, Air, and Earth; Jupiter and Sagittarius; Mercury and Virgo
- Ancients: Aided in rain-making rituals
- Druids: Used beryls for *scrying*, foretelling the future through crystal balls
- Scots: Considered beryl a stone of power
- 12th Century Europe: Insured success in courtroom litigation and in battle
- Renaissance Europe: Beryl spheres used for divination and scrying

BISBEE ICE
❖ Unique form of CALCITE found only in the area of Bisbee AZ, formerly one of the most productive sources for COPPER and copper-associated minerals. Bisbee Ice frequently approaches gem quality and can be cut as cabochons.

- Suggests calmness and tranquility, especially the depth and glacier-blue color of the crystals

BIXBITE, RED EMERALD
❖ Extremely rare red variety of BERYL, characterized by very small, often heavily included, vivid red to red-purple crystals
❖ The largest concentration of gem-quality bixbite occurs in the Wah Wah mountains of Utah
❖ Faceted specimens never exceed three carats

➤ *Bixbite*: Named for Utah collector Maynard *Bixby* + *ite* 'rock or mineral'

BLOODSTONE, HELIOTROPE
❖ Composed of PLASMA [green CHALCEDONY] intermixed with spots of red JASPER or HEMATITE
❖ Traditional birthstone for Pisces

➤ *Bloodstone*: Applies to any JASPER mottled with red spots
➤ *Heliotrope*: Greek, *heliotropion* 'sun dial', from *helios* 'sun' + *tropos* 'a turning', thus 'drawn to the sun'

- Associated with Fire; Mars; Aries, Pisces, and Libra; and the numbers 4 and 6
- Anciently, believed to stanch bleeding when held next to a wound; ameliorated blood-related disorders
- believed to stop hemorrhages
- At the crucifixion, green JASPER placed at the foot of Christ's cross; His falling blood stained the green rock red, transforming it to bloodstone
- Symbolizes flagellation and martyrdom
- 1st Century A.D., Europe: Preserves the owner's health and protects against deception
- Middle Ages: Predicts weather; has the power to bring rain
- Attracts wealth and prosperity
- Aids in litigation
- Eases labor pains
- Strengthens the body's blood-related organs and systems

BLUE QUARTZ, SAPPHIRE QUARTZ
- ❖ Coarse-grained QUARTZ aggregate
- ❖ Colored by CROCIDOLITE inclusions
- ❖ Sometimes cut and polished as ornaments

BORNITE, PEACOCK ORE, PEACOCK COPPER
- ❖ Primarily an ore or copper, but also popular as collectors' specimens because of the vivid play of colors
- ❖ Freshly broken surfaces show bright copper-red, which tarnishes to red, purple, blue, and bronze
- ❖ Usually used in small nuggets rather than as cut or shaped gems

- ➤ *Bornite*: From Ignaz von *Born*, an Austrian mineralogist + *ite* 'rock or mineral'

- Associated with Cancer and the numbers 2 and 4
- Augments joy in life by helping to release negative energy

BRAZILIANITE

- ❖ Yellow-green crystals, usually faceted
- ❖ Popular as a collectors' specimen
- ❖ Found in Brazil and in the state of New Hampshire, USA

➢ *Brazilianite*: Named for *Brazil*, the location of its discovery + *ite* 'rock or mineral'

BRONZITE [SEE ENSTATITE]

— C —

CALCITE, ICELAND SPAR

➢ Among the commonest of minerals
➢ Usually white or colorless, although frequently and variously colored by impurities
➢ Appears in the greatest variety of crystal forms of almost any minerals
➢ Massive forms include MARBLE, limestone, many stalactites and stalagmites, travertine, and chalk
➢ Often a primary component of marine shells and sponges
➢ Relatively soft, with a Mohs hardness of 3

➢ *Calcite*: Latin, *calc-, calx-* 'lime' + *ite* 'rock or part of a rock'
➢ *Dog-tooth Spar*: Variety whose crystals strongly resemble a dog's tooth
➢ *Iceland Spar*: Named for *Iceland*, its source: transparent variety
➢ *Satin Spar*: Finely fibrous variety with satiny sheen

• Associated with Air and Fire; Mercury and Virgo; Jupiter and Sagittarius
• Also associated with Water; the Moon; astrological Cancer; and the number 8
• Norse: used as a sun stone and divinatory aid
• Pennsylvania Dutch: Considered a traditional healing stone
• Aids the wearer in cleansing the body during a fast
• Helps strengthen memory
• Brings the wearer prosperity and wealth

CALIFORNITE, IDOCRASE, "CALIFORNIA JADE"

❖ Jade-like, gemstone-quality VESUVIANITE

➤ *Californite*: *California* + *ite* 'rock or part of a rock'
➤ *Idocrase*: Greek *eidos* 'form, shape' + *krasis* 'mixture'

• Enhances its wearer's patriotism and loyalty
• Ameliorates skin eruptions

CARBUNCLE

❖ Formerly used to describe any rounded, cabochon-cut gem
❖ Former name for almandite GARNET

➤ *Carbuncle*: Latin, *carbunculus* 'live coal, spark', ultimately from *carbon* 'burning charcoal' + *culus*

CARNELIAN

❖ Worked as a gem stone by 7,000 B.C.
❖ Fine-grained CHALCEDONY colored by HEMATITE
❖ Egyptians: Used as ornaments before 3,000 B.C.
❖ Traditional gemstone for Thursday

➤ *Carnelian,* also *Cornelian*: Latin, *cornum*, 'cornel berry' or 'cornelian cherry'

• Romans: Protected against fear, envy, and anger
• 13th Century Arabia: Endows its owner with courage in battle
• Brings peace and protection
• Relieves sexual tension; energizes sluggish sexual energy
• Helps staunch the flow of blood from wounds

CAIRNGORM [SEE SMOKY QUARTZ]

CASSITERITE, TIN STONE

❖ Forms bright, shiny, highly attractive black crystals

> *Cassiterite*: Greek, *kassiteros* 'tin', from Elamite, *kassi-ti-ra* 'coming from the land of Kassi' [term used by Carthaginian traders for Cornwall, in Britain, the site of the earliest and most extensive tin mines]
> *Tin*: Old English *tin,* from a probable Germanic word, *tinan*

CAT'S EYE QUARTZ
❖ Naturally occurring colorless QUARTZ containing inclusions of parallel hornblende-asbestos fibers
❖ Displays *chatoyancy* when cut as cabochons
❖ May be simulated by heat-treating TIGER'S EYE or HAWK'S EYE

> *Cat's Eye Quartz*: Name given to the natural rough
> *Quartz Cat's Eye*: Name given to the stone when cut *en cabochon*

CERUSITE, CERUSSITE, LEAD CARBONATE, WHITE-LEAD ORE
❖ Important lead ore in its granular and massive varieties
❖ Colorless, white, or yellow transparent crystals
❖ Difficult to cut because it is extremely brittle; primarily as collectors' specimens
❖ Renaissance: Whitening agent in cosmetics (occasionally with lethal results)
❖ Formerly an important ingredient in lead-based paints; ingestion caused death by lead poisoning

> *Cerusite*: Latin *ceris* 'white lead' + *ite* 'rock or mineral'; alternatively from Greek, *keros* 'wax' + *ite* 'rock or mineral', for the waxy appearance of its crystals

• Associated with Virgo and the number 2
• Helps eliminate infestations in gardens
• Inspired confidence

CHALCEDONY
See also CARNELIAN, CHALCEDONY ROSE, CHRYSOPRASE, DAMSONITE, FLINT, GARNET, JASPER, MOSS AGATE, ONYX, PLASMA, PRASE, SARD; see also QUARTZ, JASPER

- ❖ Composed of submicroscopic QUARTZ grains colored by other inclusions of minerals
- ❖ Associated with ancient Central Asian trade routes, especially in the form of intaglios, ring bezels, and beads
- ❖ Carved artifacts from the 1st century A.D. found in Afghanistan

- ➤ *Chalcedony*: Latin, *chalcedonius,* from Greek *khalkedon* 'one of the mystical stones of Revelations'; possibly derived from Khalkedon, in Asia Minor
- ➤ *Blue Chalcedony*: One of the more valuable gemstone varieties; opaque to translucent sky-blue
- ➤ *Chrome Chaldecony, Mtodorite, Mtorolite*: Trade name for a Zimbabwean green variety

- • Associated with Air and Fire; Mercury and Virgo; Jupiter and Sagittarius
- • Greeks and Romans: Heightens calm and peaceful feelings; protects the wearer while traveling; protects against negative emotions or disturbing dreams
- • Romans: Popular stone from which to carve seals
- • Europeans: Insures the wearer success in litigation; increases lactation in mothers.
- • 17th Century Europe: Protects the wearer from evil spirits and nightmares
- • Victorians: Used the many forms of chalcedony for cameos
- • Blue chalcedony promotes sleep, peaceful dreams, calm, and healing
- • Banishes fear, anxiety, depression

CHALCEDONY ROSE, DESERT ROSE
- • Insures purity and positive, enhancing dreams

CHAROITE
- ❖ Found in only one location in Eastern Siberia; deep purple stone interspersed with quartz and manganese suggesting such depth that specimens may seem artificially colored. Because of its lim-

ited source, inordinately expensive as a semi-precious stone.

❖ First discovered in 1947 in Russia but not introduced to the West until the late 1970s

❖ Occasionally, the white streaks show a distinct *chatoyancy,* or cat's-eye effect

➢ *Charoite*: Russian, *Charo* 'Charo River' + *ite* 'rock or mineral'

• Contemporary symbol for universal brotherhood

• Aids in cleansing and purifying the body

CHAROITE

Wizard-ware—twilit
Charoite invites visions
Strewn in crystal-veins

CHERT [SEE FLINT]

CHIASTOLITE

❖ Variety of ANDALUSITE found in long, opaque, grey prismatic crystals that reveal an internal cross when cut in cross-section

❖ The cross structures are composed of graphite, a form of carbon

➢ *Chiastolite*: From Greek, *khiastos*, 'crossed', from *khiazein* 'to mark with an X' + *lite* 'rock or mineral'

CHRYSOBERYL, ALEXANDRITE, CAT'S EYE

[Not identical with CAT'S EYE QUARTZ or TIGER'S EYE QUARTZ]

❖ Although known since antiquity, first identified as a species separate from BERYL in 1789

❖ *Cat's Eye*—the most outstanding example of *chatoyancy* among gemstones. Long treasured in the Orient but popular in the West only since the late 19th Century

❖ Only chrysoberyl referred to simply as "cat's eye"; all other varieties prefaced by the name of the stone, as in "quartz cat's eye"

❖ Cat's eye alexandrite occurs, but extremely rarely

❖ Alexandrite changes from red in incandescent light to green in

natural light, the outstanding example of color-change in gemstones
- ❖ Gem-quality alexandrite among the most expensive of all gemstones
- ❖ Because of its value, not frequently found in round brilliant cuts, the most stone-wasteful gemstone cut
- ❖ Largest chrysoberyl crystals found weighed over 60 carats (about ½ oz.)
- ❖ Largest alexandrite rough, from Sri Lanka, weighed 1876 carats; largest cut alexandrite, in the Smithsonian Institution in Washington D.C., weighs 67 carats
- ❖ *Alexandrite*, with PEARL and MOONSTONE, the birthstone for Gemini
- ❖ *Alexandrite*: Contemporary gemstone for June
- ❖ *Alexandrite*: Gemstone for 45th and 55th wedding anniversaries

- ➢ *Chrysos*: Greek, *khrusoberullus—khrusos* 'golden' + *beryl*
- ➢ *Alexandrite:* Named in honor Czar Alexander II, on whose birthday in 1830 the mineral was first discovered
- ➢ *Cymophane*: Greek, *kuma* 'wave' + *phanes* 'appearing'; alternate name for cat's eye chrysoberyl

- • Associated with Earth and Fire; Venus and Taurus; the Sun and Leo; Mars-Pluto and Scorpio
- • *Alexandrite*: Associated with Scorpio and Virgo and the number 5
- • Hindu: Cat's eye composes the topmost branches of the World Tree; encourages affinities with the Spirit World
- • Hindu: Cat's eye preserves health, increases longevity, and wards against poverty
- • Sri Lanka: Cat's eye protects its wearer from evil powers
- • Orient: Endows the owner with foresight when the stone is pressed against the forehead
- • 19th Century Russia: Alexandrite (named for the reigning Czar, on whose birthday in 1830 the mineral was found) brings good luck; has talismanic powers

- *Alexandrite*: Far East—associated with good luck
- *Alexandrite*: Augments the power of love spells
- *Chrysoberyl*: Protects its wearer from the evil eye

CHRYSOCOLLA
- ❖ Blue-green COPPER derivative
- ❖ Relatively soft but occasionally cut into cabochons and beads

- *Chrysocolla*: Latin, *chrysocolla,* from Greek, *chrysokolla* 'gold solder', from *chryso-* + *kola* 'glue'

- Associated with Earth and Water; Venus-Neptune and Pisces
- Ancients: Attracted love and harmony
- Held in the hand, lessens fear and instills peace
- Relieves fear and augments initiative
- Heals inflammation and disease

CHRYSOCOLLA

Pale-washed blue-in-black
Until the rock
Being struck—

Shatters
And sharp fragments
Cluster

Lazur-like
Microscopic
Pock-scapes:
　　　　Knolly meadows brightly drused with snow
　　　　Secret caverns lipped in rippled blue
　　　　Glassy moss-crusts crumbling to grit

Each spiraled twist of wrist
Or jittered lens—each flensing glint
Of light

Reveals one
Small intense spin-
Glittered crystalled Omniverse.

CHRYSOLITE
❖ Golden-yellow form of PERIDOT

➢ *Chrysolite*: Greek, *khrusoberullus—khrusos* 'yellow/golden' + -*lite* 'stone'

CHRYSOPRASE
❖ Composed of mixed JASPER and CHALCEDONY; translucent, colored green by nickel SERPENTINE
❖ Egyptians: Used as ornaments before 3,000 B.C.

➢ *Chrisoprase*: Greek, *khrusoprasos—khrusos* 'gold' + *prason* 'leek, hence green'

• 11th Century Byzantines: Assuages eye pains and protects against internal pains
• 13th Century Europe: A Thief, willing to place chrysoprase in his mouth, may escape the death sentence
• Chrysoprase crystal placed in the mouth grants invisibility
• Reduces fever and inflammation
• *Lemon Chrysoprase*: Promotes presence of mind.

CINNABAR, CINNABARITE
❖ Deep red MERCURY sulfide, used as a pigment; a natural form of vermilion
❖ Primary source for MERCURY
❖ Roman Empire: Cinnabar mined for the pigment and for the metal mercury; because mining often led to death by mercury poisoning, the Romans used convict labor in the mines
❖ Probably the oldest mine and the world's most important source, at Almaden, Spain, has been in operation for almost 2, 500 years
❖ Mayans: Cinnabar used in royal burial chambers as insets in limestone sarcophagi; its toxicity was seen as a deterrent to

would-be thieves

- ❖ China: In spite of its toxicity, powdered cinnabar traditionally mixed with water as a medicine
- ❖ In jewelry, massive cinnabar most often carved as ornaments or shaped into carved beads
- ❖ Crystals up to 2 ¾ inches long found in China

- ➢ *Cinnabar*: From Latin, *cinnabaris,* from Greek, *kinnabari,* a word of Eastern origin; alternatively, Persian, *zinjifrah* 'dragon's blood'
- ➢ *Metacinnabarite*: Black variety

- • Ancient Chinese: Crystals of cinnabar could be transformed into gold
- • Taoists: Represents the embryo of immortality, manufactured within the body as sperm
- • Clears heat from the body and tranquilizes the mind

CITRINE
- ❖ Yellow microcrystalline variety of QUARTZ
- ❖ Earliest appearances: Hellenistic Greece, circa 250 B.C.
- ❖ Frequently produced by heat-treating AMETHYST crystals
- ❖ Iron causes the yellow tint; the more iron, the deeper the color
- ❖ Birthstone for November
- ❖ Gemstone for the 17th wedding anniversary

- ➢ *Citrine*: French, *citron* 'lemon,' from Latin, *citron* 'citron tree,' after the color

- • Associated with elemental Air; with Gemini, Aries, Libra, and Leo
- • Particularly valued by ancient Celts and Scots
- • Traditionally attracts wealth and prosperity
- • Valuable in treating depression
- • Stimulates memory, creativity, and intuition
- • Strong protective talisman

- Aids in developing a clear line of thought
- Crystals help rid the body of both physical and emotional difficulties

CLINOZOISITE [SEE EPIDOTE]

COPPER

❖ An element as well as a precious metal

❖ Possibly the first metal used by human cultures, as long as 11,000 years ago, with copper tools appearing some 7,000 years ago in the Tigris-Euphrates Valley (modern Iran/Iraq)

❖ One Egyptian pyramid has a copper plumbing system that is over 5,000 years old; pyramids constructed with copper tools

❖ Iraq, China, Egypt, Sumeria, and Greece all used copper in various forms

❖ Evidence for copper in China over 4,000 years ago

❖ New World copper appears about 4,000 years ago

❖ Ancient Israel: Used in writing and preserving one of the Dead Sea Scrolls

❖ Copper and TIN, combined as bronze, one of the first metal alloys developed by human cultures about 6,000 years ago, giving its name to the Bronze Age

❖ Second only to IRON in its industrial significance

❖ One of the few metals that occur naturally as uncompounded minerals, that is, in nuggets or nodules

❖ Lake Superior copper was pure enough that it required only melting to prepare it for industrial use

❖ Malleable, ductile, and an extremely good electrical conductor

❖ In spite of its usefulness, copper is nonetheless toxic

❖ Contemporary: copper is mined in over 50 separate nations

➤ *Copper*: Greek, *Kuprios* 'from Cyprus [*Kuprus*]' source of the finest copper available to the ancient world

- Associated with Water; with the planet Venus; with Taurus and Sagittarius; and with the number 1

- One of the seven metals associated with Alchemy
- Associated with the goddess Aphrodite/Venus; considered an essentially feminine mineral
- Enhances healing
- Copper bracelets and other ornaments facilitate healing of the physical body
- Enhances plant growth
- Effects the mind and the emotions
- Empowers love spells when used in conjunction with EMERALD

COPROLITE

- ❖ "Coprolite is always good for a gasp and a giggle." – Robyn A Harton
- ❖ Coprolites may be as large as a modern stove or refrigerator (which gives one pause, considering its source)
- ❖ Range in age from the Cambrian era to recent times
- ❖ In spite of its disreputable beginnings, coprolite—particularly dinosaur coprolite—provides one of the most colorful stones in nature, especially in its range of vivid reds and greens

- ➤ *Coprolite:* Greek, *kopros*, dung + *-lite*, rock; hence, a piece of petrified or FOSSILIZED dung
- ➤ *Regurgitalith*: A related form, in that it is the fossilized remains of regurgitated stomach contents
- ➤ *Gastrolith*: A related form, that is, a stone that once formed part of the digestive systems of an animal, usually functioning in a gizzard; dinosaur gastroliths may weigh several pounds each

- Aids the wearer in being open to change and adaptable to new ideas

CORAL

- ❖ One of the few organic gemstones (along with AMBER, IVORY, JET, and PEARL)
- ❖ Earliest uses: Sumeria, circa 3,000 B.C.

- ➢ *Coral*: Greek, *korallion*, probably related to Hebrew/Semitic, *goral,* 'pebble'

- Associated with Water
- Hindus: Purifies the blood
- Greek mythology: When Perseus killed the monstrous shake-haired Medusa, the drops of her blood became coral
- Romans: Amulets protected children from danger
- Ovid, 1st Century A. D.: Effective cure for scorpion and snake bites
- 9th Century Arabia: Encourages good humor in the wearer
- 12th Century England: Talisman against enemies and wounds, especially when incised with the figure of a gorgon or a serpent
- Medieval England: Ameliorates the pains and dangers of child-birth
- Pueblo Indians: Formed animal fetishes from red coral
- Italy (to the present):Protects against the "Evil Eye"
- Carrying red or white coral allows one to control the weather
- Stops hemorrhaging
- Endows the wearer with wisdom
- New Age: Combined with DIAMOND, RUBY, EMERALD, and PEARL and hung over the entryway, forms a powerful amulet to keep a house safe and its inhabitants safe from harm
- New Age: Red coral aids in menstruation and balancing cycles
- *Black Coral*: Powerful when carved into talisman; protects the wearer from harm
- *Pink Coral*: Stimulates healing and pleasure; represents continuity and structure
- *White Coral*: Stabilizes earth-harmonies

CORDIERITE [SEE IOLITE]

CORUNDUM
- ❖ Pure corundum white to dull brown; various impurities give it

the colors that transform it into RUBY and SAPPHIRE

- ❖ Known in the Far East from antiquity; entered the West in the 18th century as powered abrasives from China
- ❖ Scratch-resistant glass, formed from corundum, serves as window glass for space craft and satellitesBest known for its gemstone varieties

- ➤ *Corundum*: Tamil, *kuruntam,* probably from Sanskrit, *kuruvinda* 'ruby'
- ➤ *Emery*: black non-gemmy corundum
- ➤ *Ruby*: Red translucent to transparent gemstone
- ➤ *Sapphire*: Translucent to transparent corundum in any color other than red

- • Associated with Air and Fire; Mercury and Virgo; Jupiter and Sagittarius; and with the number 1
- • Ancient Rome: One of seven stones worn by seafarers for protection

EAGLE

From this angle it perches
On Corundum—
Thai-ruby rough, opaque,
Corrupted, worn
Half-domed, and swirled
By dark in-
        clusions
Beneath harsh emery claws—

Star-ruby-brown,
Radiating angles from its core
Where flight embeds,
Fractures,
Re-
      flects
In metaphors that

Form then shift and then

Transform—
Next time it might grasp
Green seafoam
Froth
Or plum-
      met
On the weight of
Liquid light

CROCIDOLITE, BLUE ASBESTOS, RIEBECKITE

❖ Fibrous asbestine material that gives chatoyancy to TIGER'S EYE and HAWK'S EYE

➤ *Crocidolite:* Greek, *krokid,* 'nap, wool' + *ite* 'rock or mineral'
➤ *Riebeckite*: Named for the German explorer Emil *Riebeck* + *ite* ' rock or mineral'

- New Age: enhances wearer's mathematical abilities
- Heightens intuition and allows its wearer to distinguish between important things and over-hyped trivia

CRYSOPRASE [SEE CHRYSOPRASE]

CUBIC ZIRCONIA, CUBIC ZIRCONIUM

❖ Rare in nature but easily synthesized
❖ Originally developed for use in lasers
❖ Among the most common DIAMOND simulants; economically the most important one since the mid 1970s
❖ CZ are almost flawless; nearly all diamonds will exhibit some flaws
❖ CZ can be colorless; only the rarest and most expensive diamonds are colorless
❖ Trace elements introduced during production result in a wide range of colors
❖ By the 1980s, 50,000,000 carats produced world-wide

— D —

DAMSONITE [TRADE NAME], ARIZONITE, AMETHYSTINE CHALCEDONY

❖ A unique purple to purple-gray form of chalcedony, found primarily in Arizona

➤ *Damsonite*: Named from the color of the *Damson* plum + *ite* 'rock or mineral'

• Associated with Leo, Virgo, and Libra; and with the numbers 1 and 6
• Ancients: Considered a heart stone, aiding in honest emotions and ameliorating regret
• New Age: Instrumental in cleaning the environment and stimulating subtle energy.

DANBURITE

❖ Like TOPAZ and QUARTZ, a nearly transparent stone, but with subtle differences in luster and shape that makes it increasingly popular as a gemstone; it may be tinged with pink and yellow
❖ Frequently found in nearly perfect clusters of crystals, attractive for their wedge-shaped terminations
❖ Always displays a glassy sheen
❖ Visually its crystals resemble TOPAZ

➤ *Danburite:* Named for its first source, *Danbury* CT, in 1839; the original location has been covered by buildings

• Fills body, mind, and soul with clear, loving light

- Assists in cleansing and purification
- Encourages patience

DEMANTOID
Rare, valuable green variety of GARNET

DIAMOND
- ❖ Exhibits superlatively all of the key qualities prized in gemstones: brilliance and fire, beauty, durability, rarity, and portability
- ❖ Formed some 90 miles beneath the earth's surface, at 50,000 atmospheres of pressure
- ❖ Identical chemical composition to CARBON and graphite, differing only in crystal structure and properties
- ❖ Graphite is more stable than diamond; essentially all diamonds are in the extremely slow process of transforming into graphite
- ❖ Earliest source—unfaceted but polished stones produced in India, circa 800 B.C.; India remained the only source of diamonds for almost 2,500 years
- ❖ For centuries diamonds were not cut or re-shaped, out of fear that to do so would destroy their inherent magical qualities (and also because the technology to do so had not been developed)
- ❖ 13th Century: Louis IX of France issued an edict forbidding women to wear diamonds
- ❖ Mid-15th Century: First successful faceting of diamonds; before that time, gemstone diamonds were mounted as a natural octahedral crystal
- ❖ 15th Century: First diamond engagement ring—Hapsburg Emperor Maximilian I to Mary of Burgundy
- ❖ Mid-16th Century: *Rosette* or *rose* cut introduced in Belgium
- ❖ 17th Century: *Brilliant* or *Mazarin* cut, with 17 facets on the upper half of the stone, introduced
- ❖ 18th Century: Diamonds discovered in Brazil, breaking India's monopoly
- ❖ 19th Century: South African mines, the richest yet discovered, begin producing

- 1919: Marcel Tolkowsky applied mathematical calculations to diamond cutting, developing the modern *round brilliant* cut
- 20th Century: Australia produces the greatest quantities of diamonds
- India is the largest center for cutting diamonds
- Largest uncut crystal on display, 254 carats, Smithsonian Institution, Washington D.C.
- The world's largest rough diamond was the *Cullinan*, at 3,106.00 carats (found in South Africa in 1905); it was cut into *Cullinan I-IX* and 96 other stones; the second largest, the *Excelsior*, was a mere 995.20 carats, cut into 21 stones
- The 530.20 carat *Cullinan I*, the "Star of Africa," set in the British Royal Scepter in the Tower of London, the second largest cut diamond in the world
- The *Kohinoor*, 108.9 carats, first appeared in 1304, in the possession of the Mogul Emperor of India; its legendary history extends nearly 5,000 years
- Hardest natural substance known; 140 times the cutting resistance of CORUNDUM (RUBY and SAPPHIRE), even though they are second on the Mohs scale of hardness
- Four times harder than CORUNDUM
- Most effective conductor of heat, five times more so than second-place SILVER
- Highest melting point of any natural mineral
- Traditional gemstone of Aries
- Traditional stone of Libra
- Traditional gemstone for Sunday and Saturday

- *Diamond*: Greek, *adama, a* 'not' + *daman* 'tame, subdue, break down, conquer'—related to *adamantine*.
- *Carbonado*: Black crystalline diamond found in Brazil
- *Boart*: Industrial diamond found in Brazil and South Africa

- Associated with Earth, Air, Fire, and Water; Saturn; Uranus; Mercury and Gemini; Moon, Cancer
- Hindus, 5th Century Sanskrit manuscript: Protects its wearer by

warding against serpents, fire, poison, illness, thievery, floods, and malign spirits. Flawed stones, on the other hand, invited such calamities, as well as lameness, jaundice, and leprosy.

- Greece and Rome: Eros/Cupid used diamond-tipped arrows to ensure that those the arrows struck would fall in love
- Greece and Rome: Protects its wearer from madness and fear
- Greece and Rome: Steeping a crystal in goat's blood softened it sufficiently to be split
- Middle Ages: Considered alternatively a poison or an antidote to poison; magical stone endowed with great power.
- Europe 16th Century: Powdered diamond mixed with food considered a sure poison
- America, 20th Century: Hope Diamond, a 45.5 carat blue diamond, considered cursed jewel
- Endows its wearer with courage, strength, and invincibility in battle. "One of the counts of the indictment of the Chief Justiciar Hubert de Burgh in 1232 was that he had furtively removed from the royal treasury a gem which made its wearer invincible in battle and had bestowed it upon his sovereign's enemy, Llewellyn of Wales" (Sofianides and Harlow 20; citing Joan Evans).
- Symbolizes constancy and purity; enhances marital love. Infidelity by either partner may cause the diamond to lose its efficacy.
- Contemporary lore: A diamond received as a gift has more power than one purchased
- Stone of the mind, reflecting its hardness
- Prevents unwanted dreaming
- Brilliance forms a protective barrier against negativity

DIOPSIDE

- ❖ Bottle-green to light green, also dark brown and violet blue crystals
- ❖ Used primarily as a gemstone and as refractory material
- ❖ Important constituent of the Earth's mantle
- ❖ Occurs naturally in meteorites

- ❖ As gemstone, transparent crystals faceted; dark green to black heavily included crystals cut as cabochons or fashioned into beads

- ➤ *Diopside*: Greek, *di* 'two' + *opsis* 'appearance, sight' + *ide*
- ➤ *Chrome Diopside*: A deep, emerald green diopside, colored by chromium inclusions, and often faceted as a gemstone
- ➤ *Star Diopside*: Black diopside showing *asterism*, caused by needle-like inclusions of magnetite, manifested as a four-rayed star
- ➤ *Violane, Violan*: Name given to occasional dark blue to violet-blue crystalline or massive diopside

- • Associated with Earth and Water; Venus-Neptune/Pisces
- • Worn at the throat, attracts love into one's life
- • Excellent for Heart chakra
- • Increases the ability to trust others
- • Increases compassion for self and others
- • Ameliorates fever and aches by balancing the body's temperature

DIOPTASE
- ❖ Frequently valued as collectors' specimens because of the brilliant emerald-green crystals
- ❖ Color may be so strong that it makes crystals translucent rather than transparent and masks the fire
- ❖ Although occasionally cut into small faceted gems or cabochons, its fragility precludes its use in most forms of jewelry
- ❖ Specimens discovered in Kazakhstan, the most important historical source, were once sent to the Tsar of Russia as EMERALDS

- ➤ *Dioptase*: French, *di-, dia-* 'through' + Greek, *optasia* or *optima* 'view, see, vision', referring to its transparent crystals

- • Associated with Earth; Venus; Mercury and Virgo; Jupiter and Sagittarius
- • African Congo: A talisman of great power

- New Age: Expands the consciousness
- New Age: Dioptase represents an immature evolutionary stage; left unmined, the crystal will evolve into EMERALD Enables healing of any problems afflicting the brain

DOLOMITE

❖ Occurs as crystals, useful primarily as collectors' specimens
❖ Transparent crystals occasionally faceted
❖ Massive forms used commercially as ornamental stone, in manufacturing concrete, and as a source of magnesium oxide

➤ *Dolomite*: French, after Déodat de *Dolomieu* (1705-1801), an early geologist + *ite* 'rock or mineral'

- Ameliorates grief
- Improves digestion

DUMORTIERITE

❖ Gemstone dumortierite is commonly blue, although the stone may also be pink, green, or violet
❖ Commonly fashioned into cabochons, beads, eggs, spheres, and ornamental sculptures
❖ Crystals are pleochroic, showing red, blue, and violet depending upon the direction viewed
❖ Occasionally used to imitate LAPIS LAZULI

➤ *Dumortierite*: French, after Eugène *Dumortier*, a 19th-century French paleontologist
➤ *Denim Dumortierite*: A pale blue variant, approximating the color of stone-washed denim
➤ *Dumortierite Quartz*: Dumortierite crystals inter-grown with QUARTZ

- Ameliorates impatience and reduces excitability
- Encourages a calm, business-like response to events

— E —

EILAT STONE [SEE MALACHITE]

EMERALD

- ❖ Green to blue-green variety of BERYL
- ❖ Deep green emerald associated with Earth Mother
- ❖ Traditional birthstone for May; traditional gemstone for Taurus and Cancer
- ❖ Earliest sources: Egypt, c. 1650 B.C., so-called Cleopatra's Emerald Mines already operating
- ❖ Hebrews: Contained in the breastplate of the High Priest
- ❖ Highly valued in ancient cultures
- ❖ Traditional gemstone for Tuesday and Friday
- ❖ Carat for carat, the most valuable of gemstones
- ❖ Colored BERYL containing a small percentage of chromium
- ❖ All natural emeralds are flawed, that is, contain *inclusions* of other materials; most samples are heavily included, making gem-quality specimens rare and valuable
- ❖ In spite of myths and legends proposing Indian or Oriental sources, the finest emeralds occur primarily as crystals in the mines of Colombia, South America—there are some 100 such mines still in operation; mining in South America began over 400 years ago
- ❖ Colombian emeralds generally show the most transparency and the most fire, hence are most highly valued
- ❖ The greatest collections of emeralds is secured in the Republic of Bogota Bank in Columbia, including five crystals weighing between 220 and 1,795 carats (12 ½ oz.)
- ❖ Famous stones include:

> *Duke of Devonshire*: 1,383.95 carats, uncut; gift from Emperor Dom Pedro I of Brazil to William Spenser, 6th Duke of Devonshire, in 1831; British Museum
>
> *Gachala*: 858 carats (172 g.), 5-cm Colombian stone, uncut, discovered in 1967; Smothsonian Institution

❖ To improve clarity of included stones, most emeralds are treated with oil, often cedar oil (an acceptable treatment in most gem trades)

❖ "Created" or "lab-grown" emeralds are synthetic simulants chemically identical to naturally occurring specimen; some lab-grown emeralds display veil-like inclusions

➢ *Emerald*: Latin/Greek *smaragdos,* meaning and history unclear

➢ *Oriental Emerald*: Not a true emerald but a transparent green variety of CORUNDUM

➢ *Trapiche Emerald*: Rare variety of Colombian emerald with a six-pointed star pattern caused by radiating lines of included carbon; from Spanish, *trapiche* 'grinding wheel' used in working sugar cane

- Ruled by the Moon
- Traditional birthstone for Gemini
- 4th Century B.C.: Enables its owner to rest and relieve the eyes
- India: Used to ornament temples
- Rome: Symbolized and enhanced the reproductive forces of nature; dedicated to Venus
- Early Christians: Symbolized the Resurrection (i.e., green as the color of rebirth and renewal, spring, and growth)
- Moslems: Carved as amulets, with inscribed verses from the Koran
- 11th Century Europe: Improves memory, increases eloquence and persuasiveness, and causes joy
- 13th Century Europe: Represents an antagonist to sexual pleasure. "Albertus Magnus wrote that when King Bela of Hungary embraced his wife, his magnificent emerald broke into three pieces" (Sofianides and Harlow 63).

- 16th Century Europe: Effective ward against and/or cure for epilepsy, bleeding, fever and dysentery, and panic
- Capable of blinding snakes
- Protects against the bite of poisonous creatures
- Protects against dysentery
- Facilitates childbirth
- Endows its owner with the ability to foretell the future
- Enhances its wearer's creativity, imagination, prosperity, success in love and fertility
- Ensures that the wearer will remain faithful and loyal; thus given by one lover to another to carry when they are separated
- Considered the stone of love
- Aids in fertility, self-growth, and honesty
- Stimulates the brain and memory
- Considered to have antiseptic abilities

EMERY

❖ A non-gemstone, often impure form of CORUNDUM, frequently mixed with HEMATITE or MAGNETITE

➢ *Emery*: Middle French, *emery,* from Old French, *emery* or *esmeril, from* Italian, *smeriglo,* ultimately from Latin *smericulum*; equivalent to Greek, *smuris* 'rubbing powder'

- Associated with Saturn
- Aids in concentration and focus

ENSTATITE [ALSO BRONZITE]

❖ One source of enstatite is stony and iron meteorites, making it an *extra-terrestrial* gemstone
❖ Often used as an ornamental stone
❖ Most gem-quality material found as naturally rolled pebbles
❖ Green enstatite often found in association with DIAMONDS
❖ Tumbling, polishing, or faceting reveals its gemstone qualities
❖ Weathered enstatite with some iron included becomes lustrous

and semi-metallic, displaying an attractive *schiller*; such material is called *bronzite*

➢ *Enstatite*: From Greek *enstatēs*, 'adversary' + *ite* 'rock or mineral', referring to its high melting point, that it, it is an 'opponent' of heat

➢ *Bronzite:* Named its color + *ite* 'rock or mineral'; most specimens from Austria

➢ *Chrome-enstatite*: Emerald-green chromium-rich variety

• *Encourages the wearer to physical activity*

EPIDOTE

❖ Yellow-green to dark green crystals, often forming as a crust on other materials

❖ Particularly transparent crystals occasionally faceted as gemstones

❖ In general, however, a collector's specimen

➢ *Epidote*: Greek, *epididonai*—*epi* 'in addition' + *donai* 'to give, to increase'—so named because two sides of the crystal base are longer than the other two

➢ *Clinozoisite*: Iron-deficient white or pink variety of epidote, chemically identical to ZOISITE

➢ *Epidosite*: Rock formed of epidote and QUARTZ

➢ *Foqueite*: Variety with up to 10% iron

➢ *Piemontite, Piedmontite*: Named for *Piedmont,* a region in Italy + *ite* 'rock or mineral'; red, opaque manganese-rich variety, the finest specimens of which may be cut *en cabochon*

➢ *Tawmawite*: Deep green, chrome-rich variety from Burma

➢ *Wiothamite*: Manganese-bearing variety of piemontite

• Associated with Water; Neptune/Pisces; Virgo

• 18th Century France and England: Represents the second 'e' in 'Forever' when the word is spelled out in stones (the first letter of the stone's name representing a letter in the word or phrase)

• Attracts wealth

- Enhances confidence in one's own powers
- Increases whatever it touches, material or psychic
- Augments spiritual and emotional growth
- New Age: "Epidote has recently entered a renewed stage of ac-celerated evolutionary growth and will soon be recognized as an important assistant in the self-healing process" (Elsbeth 162).

EUCLASE
- ❖ Relatively hard (7.5 on the Mohs scale) but with a tendency to break along cleavage planes; difficult to cut
- ❖ Primarily cut as collectors' specimens
- ❖ Pale to green-blue, with the most valuable stones found in the Colombian EMERALD area

- ➤ *Euclase*: Greek *eu* 'well' + *klasis* 'breaking', hence, 'easily cleaved'

- ❖ Associated with Virgo and Sagittarius
- "Happiness Stone"—increases the wearer's sense of happiness
- Improves communication skills

EUDIALITE, EUDIALYTE
- ❖ Considered a minor gemstone because of its rarity and generally poor crystal shape; primarily a collector's specimen
- ❖ Brown, brown-red, occasionally pink translucent material

- ➤ *Eudialite*: Greek *eu* 'well, easily' + *dialytos* 'to dissolve, de-compose'

- Aids in absorbing vitamins
- Revitalizes the wearer's personal power
- Encourages harmony and balance in matters of the heart

— F —

FELDSPAR, FELSPAR
See also AMAZONITE, LABRADORITE, MOONSTONE, SUNSTONE

❖ Feldspars account for over half of the Earth's crust, but only rarely produce gem-quality materials
❖ Commercially used in producing ceramics
❖ Active ingredient in *Bon Ami* cleansing powder (because it does not scratch)
❖ When it decomposes, it forms the mineral kaolinite, a chief component of clay

➤ *Feldspar/Felspar*: German, *Feld* 'field' + *Spat* 'spar, non-metallic mineral, non-ore-bearing rock'

• Protects its wearer
• Ameliorates consequences of diabetes
• Beneficial for sufferers of emphysema

CREEKROCK

creekrock sleek-rock ticking geoLogic
time cold-moss-hung clock-intrusion fractured
cutting/jutting/rutting iced-magmatic
tears glacial tears condensed coarse-crystal hard-

ness thrusting/bursting/thirsting melting heat
compression into quartz feldspar [pink-white
plagioclase sheer orthoclase] grain-grat-
ing crush crystal into crystal into light

softness melts hardness endures inures it-

---

self to aeons weight pressure heat heat
pressure weight and shatters with unending bite
ice snow wind heat snow Wind Ice Time abate

weight thick-sediment-clothing slides away
creekrock glistens moistens enlightens day

FIBROLITE [SEE SILLIMANITE]

FLINT, CHERT

❖ Variety of opaque, non-lustrous QUARTZ
❖ Valued by earlier cultures because it sparks when struck with steel; it breaks off a particle of the metal, which is so hot from the impact that it combines with oxygen in the air to burn
❖ In geological terms, flint is chert found in chalk beds; in general usage, chert is light grey flint
❖ Anciently—especially in Stone Age cultures—widely used in forming tools and weapons, since it chips readily into sharp-edged flakes or blades
❖ 13th Century to the present: Building material for stone walls, churches, and other buildings, particularly in England
❖ In *flintlock* arms, a small piece of steel struck a piece of flint, creating the spark that ignited the black power

➢ *Flint*: Old English, *flint,* ultimately from reconstructed Indo-European *splind* 'top split or cleave'
➢ *Elf Shot, Fairy Shot*: Folkloric names for flint

• Associated with Mars
• Associated with sacredness of Fire
• Flint knives associated with magical power
• Native American cultures: considered a holy stone
• Enhances the will to survive
• Ameliorates the difficulty of cutting emotional ties
• *Elf Shot, Fairy Shot*: helps keep fairies away

FLUORITE, FLUORSPAR
- ❖ Due to impurities within crystals, occurs in a remarkable variety of colors, including colorless, purple, green, blue, brown, violet, pink, and orange, as well as multiple shades of each
- ❖ Because of its softness, scratches easily, making it unsuitable for most jewelry
- ❖ Occasionally faceted as collectors' specimens
- ❖ Gives its name to *fluorescence*, since many varieties fluoresce in ultra-violet light

- ➢ *Fluorite*: Italian *fluor,* from Latin, *fluere* 'to flow' + *ite* 'rock or part of a rock—named from its use as a flux in smelting and metallurgy
- ➢ *Derbyshire Blue John*: Blue-purple, massive crystalline fluorite widely used during the 19th Century in ornamentation; from French, *bleu et jaune* 'blue and yellow,' its characteristic colors

- • Associated with Air and Water; Mercury and Gemini; Saturn-Uranus and Aquarius; Moon and Cancer
- • New Age: Associated with the New Millennium—relates to ancestry, family, and connectedness to the Earth
- • Facilitates intuition
- • Aids mental alertness and wards mental fatigue
- • Cleanses the aura

FOSSIL, DRACONITE, WITCH STONE
- ❖ Remains or imprints of ancient organic life—plants, animals, insects, etc.—in which organic materials have been replaced by various minerals, often preserving minute, even molecule by molecule details of structure and form
- ❖ True nature of fossils not understood until the 19th century; earlier explanations included the belief that they were the remains of animals not saved in Noah's ark, that they were concretions of the devil devised to fool the gullible, or that they merely mimicked organic forms
- ❖ Oldest fossils approximately 3,800,000,000 years old

- ❖ Value as gemstones determined in part by the rarity of the organic form; by the replacement material, as in OPALIZED wood; or by distinctive colors and/or patterns

- ➢ *Fossil*: Latin, *fosillis* 'dug up', from *fossus*, past participle of *fodere* 'to dig'
- ➢ *Coprolite*: Fossilized dung
- ➢ *Draconite*: Latin, *draco* 'dragon' + *ite* 'rock or part of a rock'
- ➢ *Stromatolite*: Fossilized algae

- • Enhances longevity

MONOLITH: THE TALE AND THE TELLER

SO Amy [*Aimee*, 'beloved', broke
Gramma's heart during WWII
being pig-headed, Dad once said]
        met us

by the hardpack driveway in
Monroe, Utah, one cloudless summery day
sometime back in
        '62

and before inviting us in—almost before
requisite kissin' and huggin'
country-kin-style was done—showed us
        the rock

AND traced a knobbly fingertip on grey
furrows she claimed told pictoglyphic tales:
A&E in Eden Indian-style but secret and
        sacred

and something she was blessed with,
dream-visions and interpretations of dreams, and
the trilobites in her ears dangled in
        shadows

from her jet-black hair, in shadows against
her dusky skin that pled dark blood.

Don't spread this around, she
                    whispered

AS she segued into Hollow Earth and
Lost Ten Tribes before returning lodestone-like
to the flat black rock that told of
                    Eden

[she said] and second-served as wheel-guard
warding wanton pickups from the fresh
and fragile green of her weedless
                    garden

TRILOBITES:

AUNT AMY,
FOSSIL-HUNTING IN SOUTHERN UTAH,
CIRCA 1955

90,000,000 years add ponderous weight—
Another score (or more?)—insensate Time
Impenetrably dense, as surface freight
Accumulates—spread grain by grain, sands limn
Silicon exchange—life and stone mate,
Twine…, urged crystal-echoes form and mime
Rigid carapace, each fleshly state
Within—density and measured hardness climb—
Until—with wind and rain, with flame and ice—
Mortised coffin-joints expand—austere walls
Disintegrate—alluvium (contrite
Perhaps) compresses to prolong the game…

Then fragments into crumbled sandstone cauls
And cuff-link-mounted, lacquered trilobites.

FUCHSITE
❖ Bright green chromium-colored variety of muscovite MICA

➢ *Fuchsite*: Named for J. N. von *Fuchs*, a 19th-century German geologist + *ite* 'rock or mineral'

— G —

GALENA, LEAD GLANCE

- ❖ A primary ore of LEAD; frequently contains SILVER
- ❖ Distinctive cubic crystal forms make it a valued collector's specimen
- ❖ Used as *kohl* by ancient Egyptians, a dark cosmetic applied around the eyes to protect from the sun's glare and repel flies

- ➤ *Galena*: Latin, *galena* 'lead ore'

- • Augments harmony and balance
- • Alleviates nervous disorders
- • Reduces inflammation
- • New Age: Perfectly formed cubic crystals represent the human body in microcosm

GARNET

- ❖ Used as early as the Bronze Age as gemstones and abrasives
- ❖ Early appearances: Egypt, as gemstone, before 3,100 B.C.
- ❖ Sumer, circa 2,300 B.C.
- ❖ Sweden, circa 2,000 B.C.
- ❖ Mesoamerica: As ornaments, used by Aztecs and others, Pre-Columbian
- ❖ Occurs in all colors; significant new varieties discovered in the past several decades
- ❖ Rare blue garnet discovered as recently as the 1990s
- ❖ Occasionally the color is so deep as to make the stone opaque
- ❖ Traditional birthstone for January
- ❖ State mineral of Connecticut
- ❖ Crystals may reach 3 feet across; others weigh as much as 500

pounds

- *Garnet*: Latin, *pome granate*, referring both to the intense color and to the seed-like form; from Latin *granatus* 'grain'
- *Almandine*: Orange-red to purple-red
- *Almandite, Carbuncle, Oriental Garnet, Almandine Ruby*: Deep red, formerly a popular gemstone
- *Andradite*: Named after J. B. de *Andrada* e Silva + *ite* 'rock or mineral'; black, brown, yellow, green, red variety
- *Demantoid*: German, *demant* 'diamond' + *oid* '-like'; emerald-green andradite, among the most valuable of garnets; sometimes wrongly called *Olivine* or *Uralian emerald*, from their discovery in the Ural Mountains in 1853; highest quality specimens rival DIAMOND, RUBY, and SAPPHIRE in price
- *Grossular, Grossularite*: Latin, *grossularia*, 'gooseberry'—so called because of their shape. Colorless, orange, pink, raspberry, yellow, brown; colored by ferrous irons
- *Hessonite, Essonite, Cinnamon Stone*: Greek, *hesson* 'inferior, less', since it is softer than ZIRCON, which it resembles
- *Knorringite*: Named for Oleg von *Knorring* + *ite* 'rock or mineral'; found only under extreme pressure and associated with kimberlite pipes, it is an indicator for DIAMONDS
- *Melanite*: Black variety of andradite
- *Pyrope*: Middle English, *pirope*, from Latin, *pyropos* 'gold-bronze', from *pyr* 'fire' + *op-* 'eye'; colorless, pink shading to red, colored by iron; most popular variety of garnet
- *Rhodolite*: Greek *rhodo-* 'rose' + *lite* 'rock or mineral'
- *Sespartite*: Named from *Sesspart*, Bavaria; brown to brown-red, infrequently used in jewelry;
- *Topazolite*: Almandite variety named for its color similarity to TOPAZ + *lite* 'rock or mineral'
- *Tsavorite*: Rare, gem-quality emerald green Garnet
- *Uvarovite:* Vivid emerald green but rarely forming crystals large enough to distinguish without a microscope; from Russia and Finland
- *YAG* [yttrium aluminum garnet]: Synthetic garnet used as a gem-

stone; earlier popular as a DIAMOND simuilant

- Associated with Air and Water; Mercury and Gemini; Moon and Cancer; Saturn-Uranus and Aquarius; Virgo, Leo, and Capricorn
- Egyptians: Grossular garnet protects against crime, cures inflammation, cleanses the blood, and strengthens bones
- *Talmud*: Noah's Ark was illuminated by a large garnet
- Greeks and Romans: Garnet talisman engraved with a dragon attracts prosperity, happiness, and health
- Middle Ages: ensures faith, truth, and constancy
- 13th Century: Protects its wearer, enhances its wearer's strength; repelled insects
- 17th Century Europe: Eliminates symptoms of Melancholy
- 19th Century Europe: *Black Garnet*: Associated with mourning
- Asia: Bullets made of or tipped with garnet inflict deadlier wounds than a lead-tipped bullet (an example of Sympathetic Magic—the red of the garnet attracts the red of blood)
- Protects the home from fire and lightning
- Enhances strength by cleansing the blood; remedies hemorrhage and other disorders of the blood
- Symbolizes constancy

GASPEITE
- ❖ Bright apple-green mineral, first discovered in 1966
- ❖ Finest specimens now come from Kambalda and Widgie Mooltha, north of Perth, Australia
- ❖ Considered a 'rare' mineral, only recently becoming popular as a semi-precious gemstone

- ➢ *Gaspeite*: Named for its source location, *Gaspé* Peninsula, Lemieux Township, Gaspé-ouest, Canada + *ite* 'rock or mineral'

- The mineral is so new that there are no traditional myths or legends associated with it

GEODE

- ❖ Nodular to globular concretions having a thin inner layer of CHALCEDONY, which supports inwardly pointing crystals, usually QUARTZ varieties (especially AMETHYST) or CALCITE
- ❖ Geodes and geode slices may be artificially dyed to create vivid blues, pinks, reds, and purples
- ❖ In 2000, a geode 26 feet long and 6 feet wide was discovered in Spain

- ➢ *Geode*: Latin, *ge-* 'earth' + *ode* 'resembling', from Greek, *geoides* 'earthlike'

- • Europeans: Geodes provided habitations for elemental spirits; frequently egg-shaped geodes were associated with feminine spirit and feminine energy

GOETHITE

- ❖ In spite of its rather elegant name, goethite is a common mineral, a primary constituent of rust and of soil
- ❖ Used in paint pigments from prehistoric times, including in the famous cave paintings of Lascaux, France
- ❖ Contemporary use as iron ore, known as brown iron ore

- ➢ *Goethite*: Named in honor of Johann Wolfgang von *Goethe* (1749-1832), the German poet and dramatist + *ite* 'rock or mineral'

- • Enables the wearer to hear the Music of the Spheres—thus particularly appropriate to its name and its connection with poetry
- • Enables men to be more in touch with their masculine natures

GOLD

- ❖ An element as well as a precious metal
- ❖ Occurs in nuggets of nearly pure metal and veins within matrix rock, often QUARTZ
- ❖ Few large nuggets survive, since most were melted into ingots; among the largest known, an 82 oz. specimen found in Califor-

- ❖ Early appearances: Among the earliest metals found in human cultures, circa 3,000 B.C.
- ❖ Chemically inactive, which means that it does not rust or tarnish, one of the reasons it is almost universally valued
- ❖ Dissolved by *aqua regia*, nitric-hydrochloric acid
- ❖ Most precious of the metals; one of the ten rarest elements in the Earth's crust
- ❖ Earth's crust averages less than 1/7,000 of an ounce (0.004 g) per ton of gold
- ❖ Most malleable metal; sheets of gold can be beaten to a thinness measured by mere molecules without separating, 1/10,000 of an inch thick
- ❖ Soft enough to be scratched by a penny
- ❖ One of the best conductors, exceeded only by SILVER and COPPER
- ❖ Ancient Egyptians: discovered how to add gold to glass, to create gold ruby glass (still prized today)
- ❖ Primary uses include ornamentation and jewelry, and as monetary reserves
- ❖ Experts estimate that historically, over 1,200,000 tons of gold have been mined
- ❖ California alone has produced between $2,000,000,000 and $3,000,000,000 worth, almost 2/3 of that amount from placer mining
- ❖ QUARTZ included with gold often cut *en cabochon*, but may be relatively expensive, since price depends upon the current market value of the gold
- ❖ Associated with the 50th wedding anniversary and other 50th jubilees

- ➢ *Gold*: Old English, *gold*, from the probable Germanic, *gulthum*, 'gold'
- ➢ *AU*, chemical symbol for gold: from Latin, *aurum*, 'shining dawn'

- Frequently considered magical by earlier cultures
- The biblical Golden Calf symbolized greed, disobedience, and evil
- Goal of Medieval alchemists, who sought to transmute less valuable 'base' metals into gold
- Middle Ages: Golden crown symbolized the king's power as analogous to the light of the Sun and the light of Heaven
- One of the seven metals associated with Alchemy—highest of all the metals, representing Fire and purification; King of metals, analogous to the Sun
- Middle Ages/Renaissance: Treatment for multiple disorders. Physicians might make an incision, insert a small gold pipe (less commonly SILVER), and keep the wound open and flowing in order to release evil 'humours' from the patient's body
- Powerful healer
- Insures wealth and wisdom
- Ameliorates the pain of arthritis for its wearer
- In wedding rings, symbolizes a long-lasting and unchanging relationship

ALCHEMY

Bare-backed Ray, tan and dirt mingling on skin
years used to summer heat; Cleta, shorts and
fifties' playsuit-top, hair wild, uncombed, sun-
streaked; me, shorts belling over skinny tanned

legs. We three clustered around the old buck-
board--splintery and splintered wreckage years
past any usefulness; we three conducting
secret tests far from prying eyes or ears

(while Grandma watched through age-bleached
    kitchen shades
and Grandpa from the shed); we three transforming
oily slicks in old Xerex cans to gold,

cooking wine from honeysuckle berries.

We prepubescent artists in chemistry—
And now transmuted by time's harsh alchemy.

GOLD

Gold flakes on quartz:
    Whispered self-atonement for
        Centuries-long greed

GOLDSTONE, BLUE GOLDSTONE, GREEN GOLDSTONE

* ❖ A man-made semi-precious stone, designed to imitate the color and flash of SUNSTONE (gem-quality form of FELDSPAR)
* ❖ Composed of COPPER inclusions in a glass groundmass
* ❖ *Goldstone*, originally using brown glass as a matrix, extends at least back to the Renaissance
* ❖ Modern *Goldstone* is also available in deep blue and hunter green

* • Augments wisdom and science
* • Because of its copper inclusions, *Goldstone* energizes
* • *Blue Goldstone* suggests cosmic distances and powers

GOSHENITE

* ❖ Colorless, transparent variety of BERYL
* ❖ All other BERYLS are colored by impurities
* ❖ *Goshenite*: Named for *Goshen,* Massachusetts, near where it was found

GYPSUM, ALABASTER

* ➢ Finely grained, often white, translucent, valued as a carving material for ornaments, particularly vases and boxes

* ➢ *Gypsum*: Greek, *gupsos,* related to Semitic/Hebrew, *gephes*

'plaster'

➢ *Alabaster*: From Latin, *alabaster*, from Greek, *alabastros* 'vase for perfumes'; possibly from Egyptian, *a-labaste* 'vessel of the goddess Bast'

➢ *Oriental Alabaster*: Misnomer for a variety of fine-grained, translucent, often banded CALCITE

- Associated with Earth and Water; Venus-Neptune/Pisces
- Associated with Water and Aries
- Ancient Egyptians: Salmon-colored eggs of gypsum symbolize fertility
- Brings the wearer prosperity

— H —

HALITE, ROCK SALT

❖ Crystallizes as an evaporate, remnant of ancient seas and salt lakes

❖ Historically valued as a savoring and a preservative; anciently valued as a trade item

❖ Ancient Rome: Soldiers paid with salt, reflected in the modern word *salary*, from Latin *salarium* 'paid in salt'

❖ Revolutionary War: Salt figured as a strategic objective when British forces tried to intercept salt supplies and thus destroy the Colonies' ability to preserve food

❖ Forms cubic crystals, usually white but also pink, light blue, and dark blue, that make attractive specimens; but best known for its use as table salt

➢ *Halite*: Latin, *halites,* from Greek, *hals* 'salt' + *ite* 'rock or mineral'

➢ *Halite Flowers*: Stalactites formed of curling halite fibers, found in Australia

• Associated with Fire; Jupiter and Sagittarius; Moon and Cancer; Mercury and Gemini; Saturn-Uranus and Aquarius; and the number 1

• Provides protection when placed in the four cardinal corners of the house

• Useful in cleansing spells

• *Blue Halite*: Facilitates finding one's soul-mate

• *Pink Halite:* Intensifies spirituality

HAWK'S EYE [SEE TIGER'S EYE, QUARTZ]
HELIODOR

❖ A BERYL variety identical to emerald except for its color, a rich yellow to yellow-green to gold

➤ *Heliodor*: Greek, *heliodorus*, from *helio* 'sun' + *doron* 'gift'—so named because of its color

• Medieval Europe: Cures laziness
• Encourages nurturing and caring

HELIOTROPE [SEE BLOODSTONE]
HEMATITE, HÆMATITE [SEE IRON]

❖ Principle iron-bearing ore
❖ Associated with blood because of its red streak and because water used in cutting and finishing hematite is stained deep red
❖ Anciently used as a pigment, ocher
❖ Probably used by the earliest societies
❖ Source of polishing rouge
❖ Recently discovered on Mars
❖ Popular among the 29th-century Victorians as jewelry; more recently popular in Southwest-style jewelry
❖ Most hematite available today is synthetic, sometimes called by the trade names "Hemalyke" and "Hematine"; difficult to distinguish from naturally occurring material, synthetic hematite is plentiful and relatively inexpensive

➤ *Hematite*: Greek, *haimatites* 'blood-red stone', from *haima* 'blood' + *ite* 'rock or part of a rock'
➤ *Iron Rose*: Name given to circular arrangements of hematite blades
➤ *Kidney Ore*: Name given to reniform (that is, kidney-shaped) deposits
➤ *Rainbow Hematite*: Iridescent in shades of blue, green, and gold
➤ *Specular Hematite, Specularite*: Displays a metallic luster

- ➤ *Tiger Iron*: Layered bands of hematite and red JASPER
- ➤ Biblical name: 'Bloodstone,' because of its red streak

- Associated with Capricorn, Aries, and Aquarius; considered Saturn's stone; associated with the number 9
- Anciently: Believed to have formed from warriors' blood spilled on battle grounds
- Egyptian: Essential element in creating magical amulets, especially those intended for headrests and heart amulets
- Egyptian: Useful in treating madness and inflammation
- Roman: The stone of Mars, god of War
- Roman: Because of its streak and its association with Mars, protects warriors in battle
- Native American: Source for red ochre paint, used as face paint and in religious ceremonies
- Heals anemia
- Stimulates courageous behavior
- Enhances self-confidence and self-esteem
- May be efficacious to women in regulating irregular menses
- *Magnetic Hematite*: Symbolizes the closeness of love as one stone is drawn to another; to kiss immediately after seeing magnetic Hematite insures enduring love.

HÆMATITE

eagle-flight   light-/height-/flight-ed fantasy
azure/pleasure   leisure feather-lilted
shifting cloudbanks   shifting ice-crushed Ecstasy
upward soaring flaring faring   jilted-

jolted-folded earthward   wingSinging harsh
airbursts fragmentary EchoSong   long
lost now   glossed now to mere memory   brash
flash/slash of eagle-gray suspended   hung

breath-length eye-blink   then sinking further/farther

Azure transmogrified as SilverBlack
flecks of fire/heat/blood   condensed-ice ardor
frailing dream/scream of flight in   crystalled slack

crimson-crystalled water weeps FloodMoans—
weeps and wets   glints/cuts/abrades BloodStone

HERKIMER DIAMOND, LITTLE FALLS DIAMONDS

❖ Misnomer given to a distinctive double-terminated form of QUARTZ crystal
❖ Almost always found in small *vugs* or pockets in the matrix stone
❖ Range from transparent to cloud and may include *phantoms, enhydro crystals,* and *scepters*

➤ *Herkimer Diamond*: Named after *Herkimer* County, NY, where it was first discovered in the late 1700s
➤ *Little Falls Diamond*: Official mineralogical name for the crystals found within the Little Falls Dolostone

• Same powers attributed to Herkimer diamonds as to any other clear crystal, but augmented in power because of the double terminations
• Aids in remembering dreams

HESSONITE [SEE GARNET]

HIDDENITE

❖ Pale to deep-green variety of SPODUMENE
❖ Most cut gemstones relatively small, generally under 2 carats

➤ *Hiddenite*: Named for geologist William Earl *Hidden* + *ite* 'rock or mineral'; community near the place of discovery later renamed "Hiddenite"

• Enhances spiritual awareness

HOWLITE

❖ Frequently dyed and used as a TURQUOISE stimulant, particularly because of its dark grey or black veining

➢ *Howlite*: Named for its discoverer, last name *How* + *lite* 'rock or mineral'

- Associated with Earth and Water; Venus-Neptune/Pisces
- Traditionally enhances memory
- New Age: Cleanses the mind of negative thoughts
- New Age: "This stone functions best when placed on a table or shelf, in close proximity to a well-frequented area" (Elsbeth 167)
- Brings ideas into sharper focus

— I —

ICELAND SPAR [SEE CALCITE]

IDOCRASE [SEE CALIFORNITE, VESUVIANITE]

IOLITE, CORDIERITE, DICHROITE

❖ Among the strongly *dichroic* minerals; that is, it changes colors depending upon the direction in which it is viewed; a fragment of violet-blue iolite may shift to blue-gray when rotated so that light strikes the crystal from a different angle
❖ Most gem-quality stones found as water-tumbled pebbles in gem gravels, most often in Sri Lanka and Burma
❖ Massive grey iolite used for carving and ornaments
❖ Principal component of the ceramic used in catalytic converters

➢ *Iolite*: Greek *ion,* 'violet' + *lite*, 'rock'; after the predominant color of the transparent gem variety
➢ *Bloodshot Iolite*: Heavily included with HEMATITE and GOETHITE, resulting in a deep red color
➢ *Cordierite*: Named after the French geologist, Pierre Louis Antoine *Cordier* + *ite*, 'rock or mineral'
➢ *Water Sapphire*: Earlier misnomer for iolite

• Traditionally enhances willingness and ability to accept responsibility
• Used by shamans to enhance healing and visions
• Believed efficacious in healing sore throats, fevers, and malaria

IRON [SEE HEMATITE]

❖ The fourth most abundant constituent of the Earth's crust and probably the major material in its core

- ❖ Identified in the Sun, in asteroids, and in distant stars; Mars may appear as the "Red Planet" because of iron oxides in its soil
- ❖ The oldest known shaped iron artifact—a dagger—made by the Hittites almost 3,500 years ago
- ❖ An iron pillar in India still stands after nearly 1,600 years
- ❖ Iron mixed with the proper proportion of carbon becomes steel, a much stronger material
- ❖ Iron found in hemoglobin is crucial to providing oxygen to cells

- ➢ *Iron*: Old English, *iren*, a later form of *isern, isen*; early forms of the word in many languages relate to "holy metal," "strong metal," "powerful," "strong"

- • One of the seven metals associated with Alchemy
- • Symbolizes the planet Mars
- • Moroccans: Wards against demons
- • Iron dagger placed beneath a sick person's pillow aids healing

IRON EYE [SEE TIGER'S EYE, QUARTZ]

IVORY

- ❖ One of the few organic gemstones (along with AMBER, CORAL, JET, and PEARL)
- ❖ Anciently: Carvings on mammoth ivory over 30,000 years old found in caves in France
- ❖ 13th Century: Used for carving in China and Europe
- ❖ Japan: Considered a precious material
- ❖ May be either recent or fossilized
- ❖ When used in jewelry, usually from the tusks of the Indian and African elephant, walrus, narwhal, and boar; and the teeth of hippopotamus and sperm whale
- ❖ Earlier used in fabricating piano keys, combs, billiard balls, and rulers
- ❖ International restrictions now curtail trade and exportation/importation of new ivory
- ❖ Widely imitated with plastics, bone, deer-horn, and vegetable ivory

- ➢ *Ivory*: From Old French *ivurie,* from Latin *eboreus* 'ivory'
- ➢ *Vegetable Ivory*: Material from the seed of certain palm trees grown in Peru and central Africa

- • Symbolizes purity

— J —

JADE

- ❖ Common name for either of two gemstone materials: nephrite (the more common, waxy-looking) and jadeite (the rarer, more translucent variety); the two varieties not related in chemical composition
- ❖ The two forms not differentiated until 1863
- ❖ Nephrite is one of the most durable substances known, hence the high value of gem-quality materials
- ❖ Earliest sources for nephrite: China, nearly 5,000 years ago; known as *yu*, the royal gem
- ❖ Earliest sources for jadeite: Olmecs, Mayas, Toltecs, and other Mesoamerican cultures, circa 1500 B.C.
- ❖ Considered by pre-Columbian Mesoamerican cultures as the most desirable and most valuable of gems
- ❖ New Zealand: Maoris began using nephrite for tools and weapons, circa 1000 A.D.
- ❖ Stone Age cultures used jade for axe heads, knives, and other weapons; later it became prized as ornamentation
- ❖ Official gemstone of Alaska
- ❖ State Official gemstone of British Columbia
- ❖ The South Island of New Zealand is called *Te Wahi Pounamu* in Maori, meaning 'The Place of Greenstone'
- ❖ Many stones marketed as 'jade' or jade simulants, including: AVENTURINE QUARTZ, CARNELIAN, CHRYSOPRASE, glass, grossularite, SERPENTINE, SOAPSTONE, VESUVIANITE, and others

- ➤ *Jade*: mistakenly applied in the 17th Century to Oriental gemstones; the name derives from the Spanish *piedra de yjada,* 'stone of the loins,' applied to Mesoamerican forms of jade in the 16th Century. French translations altered the name to *pierre le jade*

> *Chloromelanite*: Latin, *chloro* 'green' + *melan-* 'black, dark' + *ite* 'rock or mineral'; green jadeite with irregular black spots; jadeite, diopside, and acmite
> *Imperial Jade*: Burmese jadeite, emerald-green, cut in cabochons with thin, translucent edges; most desired variety of jade
> *Indian Jade*: Misnomer for AVENTURINE
> *Jadeite*: Accurate name for the Mesoamerican gemstone and others of the same composition.
> *Mutton Fat Jade*: Chinese name for a creamy white variety of jade
> *Nephrite*: From Latin *lapis nephrictus*, 'stone of the loins'; appropriate name for Chinese gemstone varieties. Nephrite is one of the most durable substances known, hence the high value of gem-quality materials
> *Pounamu*: Maori name for nephrite jade
> *Quetzal Jade*: Vivid green jadeite prized by Mesoamerican cultures
> *Russian Jade*: Variety of spinach-green nephrite from near Lake Baikal, Russia
> *Wyoming Jade*: Trade name for nephrite from Wyoming; colors include green and pink

- Associated with Earth and Water; Venus-Neptune and Pisces
- Associated with Aries, Gemini, Taurus, and Libra; and the number 11
- Ancient China: Drinking an infusion of jade, rice, and dew augments the strength of muscles and bones, purifies blood, and tones flesh. Prolonged use leads to increased endurance of heat, cold, hunger, thirst.
- Ancient China: Insures the wearer a long and prosperous life
- Ancient China: when interred with a body, jade prevented decomposition; in some instances, complete burial suits were created of jade

- Ancient China: Associated with the five cardinal virtues—charity, modesty, courage, justice, wisdom
- Ancient Egypt: Potent healer
- Ancient Mesoamerica [especially Mayas and Aztecs]: Stone of magic, associated with priests, kings, and gods
- Mayans: Referred to as "Sovereign of Harmony"
- Ancient Mesoamerica: Associated with Xiuhtecuhtli, Aztec God of Fire
- Ancient Mesoamerica: Jade placed in the mouth of a high-ranking corpse functioned as the heart in the after-life
- Ancient Mesoamerica: Powdered jade, mixed with other substances, cured fever, healed fractured skulls, and forestalled death
- Maori culture: Implements, especially weapons, of jade possessed *mana,* a quasi-magical force inspiring awe and wonder
- Renaissance Europe: A jade talisman was worn near the kidney for protection—another indication of the connections between the stone and its Latin name, which means 'kidney-stone'
- Attracts wealth
- Brings its wearer prosperity, luck, and wisdom
- Sea-green stones have a calming effect on the wearer; relieves anxiety, tension, depression
- Secures the foundation for true friendship
- Jade placed under the pillow encourages focused dreaming
- *Imperial Jade*: Potent remedy for all renal disorders

JASPER [SEE ALSO BLOODSTONE, CHRYSOPRASE; QUARTZ, CHALCEDONY]

❖ Differs from CHALCEDONY only in the arrangement of its submicroscopic QUARTZ crystals
❖ In general, jasper is opaque, AGATE is translucent
❖ Most common colors include red, yellow, and brown
❖ Earliest appearances: Paleolithic cultures

- ❖ At one time popular for use in making snuff boxes
- ❖ Gemstone of the Rooster in the Chinese zodiac
- ❖ Traditional gemstone for March in certain ancient cultures

- ➤ *Jasper*: Greek, *iaspis* 'spotted stone', ultimately of Oriental origin but meaning unknown
- ➤ *Agate Jasper*: Blended with AGATE
- ➤ *Australian Jasper*: Speckled red and light grey.
- ➤ *Basanite* Fine-grained black variety
- ➤ *Brecciated Jasper*: Jasper that has been fragmented and re-formed
- ➤ *Bruneau Jasper*: Brown, reddish brown, and cream jasper from the Bruneau River Canyon, Owyhee County, Idaho; no longer in production and difficult to locate
- ➤ *Chrysanthemum Stone*: Reddish-brown with star-shaped light to tan inclusions
- ➤ *ChrysoJasper*: Colored blue by CHRYSOCOLLA.
- ➤ *Dalmatian Jasper*: Scattered black spots on a cream to grey-white background, suggesting the coloration of Dalmation dogs
- ➤ *Egyptian Jasper*: Deep yellow and red
- ➤ *Elephant Jasper*: Brown with small black dendrites that create a spider-weblike pattern.
- ➤ *Frogskin Jasper*: Gray-tan with irregular green patterns; from Chihuahua, Mexico.
- ➤ *Heliotrope*: Bloodstone, including small inclusions of red jasper
- ➤ *Hornstone*: Fine-grained grey or reddish-brown variety
- ➤ *Imperial Jasper*: Green and yellow Mexican Jasper, partially translucent
- ➤ *Iolanthite*: Common name for banded red jasper from Crooked River, Oregon.

- *Leopardskin Jasper, Leopard Jasper*: buff to orange-tan with irregularly placed brown to black spots or rings, usually about 1/4 inch around, patterned to resemble leopards' coats.

- *Morrisonite*: Market name for a varicolored jasper, including blue/turquoise, creams, and yellows, from near Lake Owyhee, Oregon

- *Moukaite*: Red, pink, yellow, brown patterned jasper from Mooka Station, Australia.

- *Nunkirchner Jasper*: Named for a location in the Rhineland; white-grey; when dyed Berliner blue, referred to as *German lapis* or *Swiss lapis* and substitutes for LAPIS LAZULI

- *Ocean Jasper*: Vari-colored jasper, often displaying orbicular markings in green, tan, and white; occasionally displaying tiny crystal-lined vugs; relatively recent find from Madagascar

- *Oolitic Red Jasper*: Hematitic jasper containing minute rounded concretions

- *Orbicular Jasper*: Irregularly spaced orbicules, or spheres of color, that contrast with the main colors

- *Owyhee Jasper*: Trade name for orbicular jasper

- *Petrified Wood*: Much petrified wood is primarily jasper

- *Picasso Jasper*: Patterned in tan, grey, and brown, with black lines, suggesting when cut appropriately abstract paintings

- *Picture Jasper*: Beautifully patterned jasper in browns, blues, greys, often cut and polished to suggest desert landscapes

- *Poppy Jasper, Poppy Stone*: Common names for orbicular jasper with red, orange or yellow orbicules against a yellowish green background,

- *Red Jasper*: Generally uniformly colored a vivid, deep brick red; occasionally displays small PYRITEinclusions

- *Riband Jasper, Ribbon Jasper*: Banded in different colors.

- *Rogueite*: Green jasper from the Rogue River, Oregon.

- ➢ *Scenic Jasper, Picture Jasper*: Light tan with dark brown lines that, when cut appropriately, suggest natural landscapes
- ➢ *Silex*: Yellow and brownish red spotted or striped
- ➢ *Zebra Jasper*: Dark brown with light brown to nearly white streaks, from India and South Africa.

- • Associated with Virgo
- • Egyptians: Enhances the body's healing properties, especially relating to digestion
- • Provides the wearer protection, strength, and courage
- • Aids in Native rituals associated with rain-making
- • Cures snake bite
- • Aids the wearer in breaking bad habits
- • Helps balance thought proves, encouraging healthy and positive thoughts
- • Protects mother and child during childbirth
- • *Red Jasper*: Aids in lowering fevers
- • *Red Jasper*: Enhances its wearer's archery skills
- • *Green Jasper*: Aids digestive problems when inscribed with appropriate symbols
- • *Green Jasper*: Helps prevent illness
- • *Yellow Jasper*: Clears the mind
- • *Brown Jasper*: Aids in concentration

JET
- ❖ One of the few organic gemstones (along with AMBER, CORAL, IVORY, and PEARL)
- ❖ Not a mineral but a mineraloid
- ❖ Dark brown to black variety of lignite, a low-grade organic coal, in rocks of marine origin
- ❖ Prehistory: Burial artifacts made of jet
- ❖ Early appearances: Germany, circa 10,000 B.C.; England, circa 2,500 B.C.; Rome, as early as 1,400 B.C.

- ❖ Used during the 19th Century in mourning jewelry to commemorate the dead, made popular by Queen Victoria's long period of mourning for Prince Albert (from his death in 1861 until her own death in 1901)
- ❖ Whitby, on the Yorkshire coast, provided much of the Victorian jet; it has been a primary source of the mineral since the Roman occupation, before the time of Christ
- ❖ Comfortable as a gemstone since it is unusually light

- ➢ *Jet*: Middle English, *geet, jeet*, ultimately from Greek *gagates* 'stone of Gagai', a town in Syria
- ➢ *Black Amber*: Alternative name for jet, since it may produce static electricity when rubbed, as does AMBER
- ➢ *Paris Jet*: Misnomer for a variety of black glass

- • Provides protection for seafarers
- • 10th Century Spain: When carved in the shape of a human hand, Jet drives away the Evil Eye
- • 11th Century: Eliminates threat from wild beasts
- • Powdered Jet added to wine or water serves as a medication
- • Alerts the wearer to potential pitfalls and facilitates finding solutions to them

— K —

KORNERUPINE
- ❖ Rare boro-silicate first found in Greenland in 1884, valued primarily as a gemstone
- ❖ *Pleochroic*: shows green and reddish-brown when viewed from different directions
- ❖ Generally found as rounded pebbles in gem gravels
- ❖ Gemstone varieties translucent yellow to green, with deep green the most desirable
- ❖ Because of its rarity, usually faceted as collectors' specimens

- ➢ *Kornerupine*: Named for Andreas Nikolas *Kornerup*, a Danish geologist

- • Facilitates communication

KUNZITE
- ❖ Transparent pink to lilac gemstone variety of SPODUMENE
- ❖ Source of lithium
- ❖ Largest faceted specimen, 880 carats, Smothsonian institution, Washington D.C.

- ➢ *Kunzite*: Named for George Frederick *Kunz*, American gemologist (and chief buyer for Tiffany & Company) + *ite* 'rock or mineral'

- • Associated with Earth; Venus and Pluto; Scorpio, Taurus, and Libra; and the number 7
- • Enables wearers to accept things beyond their control
- • Considered a quintessentially feminine stone
- • Rejuvenates the skin and strengthens the heart
- • Helps regulate the menstrual cycle
- • Ameliorates stress and anger

- Protects against negative energies

KYANITE, CYANITE

❖ Identical in composition to ANDALUSITE and SILLIMANITE, differing in crystal structure

❖ Crystals are pleochroic, showing differing intensities of color when view from different directions

❖ Unique in that it shows a range of hardness within the same crystal (*anisotropismi*); 4.5 when scratched parallel to the long axis, 6.5 when scratched perpendicular to the axis

❖ In addition to its use as a gemstone and as collectors' specimens, kyanite is used in making spark plugs, porcelain and ceramics, and electrical insulators

➢ *Kyanite:* Greek, *kuanos* 'dark blue enamel' + *ite* 'rock or mineral'

- One of two stones than never need cleaning for use in healing
- Augments serenity
- New Age: Ideal for aligning charkas
- New Age: Stimulates meditation and dream recall
- New Age: Augments psychic awareness
- *Black Kyanite* facilitates channeling astral beings
- *Green Kyanite* gives wearers a sense of well-being

— L —

LABRADORITE, SPECTROLITE

❖ A variety of plagioclase FELDSPAR, one of the few accepted as a gemstone

❖ The finest specimens show a distinct *schiller*, sometimes called *labradorescence*, a beautiful play of green, gold, yellow, red, purple, and blue iridescence

❖ *Spectrolite*, a hard, rare form of labradorite, iridesces in a spectrum from blue to red

❖ "A man is like a bit of labrador spar, which has no luster as you turn it in your hand until you come to a particular angle; then it shows deep and beautiful colors" (Ralph Waldo Emerson; cited in Sofianides and Harlow 126)

➤ *Labradorite*: From *Labrador* (northwestern Canada), where it was found + *ite* 'rock or mineral'

➤ *Schiller*: The unique color flash associated with labradorite, also called *labradorescence*; from German, *schiller* 'iridescence', ultimately from Old high German, *scilhen* 'to wink, to blink'

➤ *Spectrolite*: Named by Professor Aarne Laitakari

• Provides courage, balance, and harmony in the face of change

• Facilitates making wise decisions

• Protects the immune system and helps replenish diminished strength

THE WAY A STONE

The way a stone
Returned to me
A glance of foam

From a stormy sea

Revealed the weave
Of Nature's grace
On a grief-filled eve
To a tear-stained face.

LAPIS LAZULI

❖ Rock, not mineral; member of the SODALITE group, composed of SODALITE and LAZURITE (25-40%), often with PYRITE and CALCITE inclusions

❖ Most probably the earliest blue gemstone

❖ Active mining began in Afghanistan (the most important producer of the aggregate) circa 3,000 B.C.

❖ Egypt: Ground into powder, lapis was used as eye-shadow—one of the first cosmetics, circa 3,000 B.C.

❖ Ancient Hebrews: One of the gemstones in the breastplate of Aaron, the High Priest

❖ Source of blue (ultramarine) pigment for painting until the mid-19th Century

❖ Several contemporary simulants available

❖ Traditional birthstone for December

➢ Greeks and Romans: Refer to lapis as *sapphirus*, a quasi-generic name for any blue stone

➢ *Lapis Lazuli*: Greek, *lapis,* 'rock, stone' + Latin, *lazulus* 'blue stone'; from ancient Persian, *Lazhuward* 'blue' and Arabic *Lazaward,* 'blue,' 'sky'; literally, *blue rock*

➢ *Lazurite*: Latin, *lazulus* 'blue stone' + *ite* 'rock or mineral'

• Associated with Water; Moon and Cancer; Mercury and Gemini; Saturn-Uranus and Aquarius

• Associated with Sagittarius and the number 3

• Babylonians, Assyrians, Egyptians: Important source of magical power, especially when carved into animal-shaped talismans

• Egyptians: Symbol for the "seat of life" when carved as heart-shaped talisman; instrumental in resurrection after death

- Egyptians: *The Book of the Dead* includes a lapis amulet in the form of an Eye to guard against evil
- Egyptians: Held the stone sacred to the goddess Isis
- Egyptians: Considered it the "Stone of Heaven"
- Buddhists: Ensures peace of mind and calm; dispels evil thoughts
- Greeks: Provides an antidote for snakebite
- Far East: Holy stone with magical powers
- 13th Century: Alleviates fever and melancholy
- 15th Century Italy: Blue, the color associated with Jupiter
- Protects the wearer from evil
- New Age: Cures depression, sadness, and grief
- Stone of truth and friendship
- Facilitates harmony in relationships
- Calms intense emotions
- Initiates the wearer's spiritual rebirth
- Acts as a channel for positive thoughts
- Powerful in developing confidence and inner strength
- Promotes fidelity in marriage

LAPIS TEARDROPS

Lapis teardrops
    Glow in gleaming twilight—
        Winged scarabs iridesce.

SOULS OF PHARAOHS

Souls of Pharaohs speak
Desiccated whisperings—
Winged scarabs whirr

LAPIS NEVADA [SEE NEVADA LAPIS]

LARIMAR, LORIMAR
- ❖ Rare form of pale to sky blue pectolite valued as a gemstone
- ❖ Known only from a single outcropping in the Dominican Republic; the single mountain now contains nearly 2000 separate mining shafts
- ❖ *Photosensitive*, which means that the color may fade with continued exposure to light

- ➢ *Larimar*: From *Larissa*, the name of the discoverer's daughter + Spanish, *mar* 'sea', for the color of the nearby Carribean
- ➢ *Pectolite*: Greek, *pektos* 'made solid' + *lite* 'rock or mineral'
- ➢ *Volcanic Blue*: Deep blue variety

- • Signifies eternal love
- • Failing that, allows participants in a divorce to remain friends

LAVA [SEE VOLCANIC ROCKS]

LAZULITE
- ❖ Visually resembles LAZURITE
- ❖ Rarely found in crystals; more common massive and granular forms frequently polished as eggs or tumbled as beads

- ➢ *Lazulite*: Latin, *lazulum*, from Arabic, *lazaward* 'blue'

- • Associated with Sagittarius and Gemini, and with the number 7
- • Helps to overcome obsessive behavior
- • Efficacious as a worry stone

LAZURITE
- ❖ Primary component of LAPIS LAZULI

- ➢ *Lazurite*: Latin, *lazulus* 'blue stone' + *ite* 'rock or mineral'

LAZURITE

For Scott and Kristine
In Memory of Charlie Ben
8/17/2000

I worked today with Lazurite—
A ragged chunk of worthless-seeming rock

Dust-grey and rough,

And only to the patient eye
Of one who cared might it reveal—beneath
Its chalky coat—an instant

Glimpse of something more.
I held it for a while, studied cracks and crags
Deciding where to use—

Judiciously, I hoped—
Hammer, chisel, fine-tipped tools
To create from one

A multitude of
Possibilities. It took a while. My hands
Grew damp from

Their long imprisonment
In heavy canvas gloves that restricted
Movement but

Protected from the random
Flash of stone. Sweat beaded on my forehead
Dripped across

Protective lenses. The
Tabletop grew grey-with-hints-of-blue.
But at the last the task

Was finished. The lazurite
Lay readied for the final stage, the polishing
That might release…,

Well, who knew what for sure.
I took the smaller fragments, remnants
Of the larger, coarser

Rock, and set them in
The tumbler, watched pure water wash
Away the last remaining

Streaks of dust, watched

The thirsty stone absorb cool moisture and transform,
Reveal

Rich subtleties of indigo,
And sapphire, and of lapis—*Lazaward, 'blue-sky'*—
Resting in its heart.

LEAD [SEE ALSO ANGLESITE, CERUSSITE, GALENA]

❖ Among the oldest metals used in human cultures
❖ Known to ancient Babylonians and first-dynasty Egyptians about 5400 years ago
❖ Used by Romans for plumbing, writing sheets, occasional coins, and cooking utensils
❖ One of the first metals used in North America, primarily as shot for firearms
❖ Most important contemporary uses, manufacturing of lead-acid batteries
❖ Shields against x-rays and nuclear radiation
❖ Cumulative poison which the body cannot expel; hence toxicity due to lead poisoning
❖ Particularly dangerous to women's reproductive systems
❖ By 2005, China the source for nearly 1/3 of the world's output

➤ *Lead*: Old English, *lead,* from Germanic, *lauda* 'lead'
➤ *Pb*: Latin symbol for the element lead, from *plumbum*; hence, *plumber,* one who works with lead pipes, originally used in plumbing

• One of the seven metals associated with Alchemy
• Symbolizes the planet Saturn
• Middle Ages and early Renaissance: Raw material capable of transmutation into gold

LEPIDOLITE

❖ Lithium-based variety of MICA, occurring in lilac, rose, pink, and gray masses
❖ Particularly attractive specimens, frequently from California, include crystals of rubellite TOURMALINE
❖ Commercially a source of lithium, rubidium, and cesium

➢ *Lepidolite*: Greek, *lepido-* 'scale, flake' + *lite* 'rock or mineral'

• Associated with Water; Jupiter and Neptune; Libra; and the number 8
• Encourages calming and revitalizing sleep
• Helps eliminate anger and negative feelings
• Helps relieve stress
• Facilitates psychic awareness
• Efficacious as a dream stone to help forestall nightmares

LODESTONE [SEE MAGNETITE]

— M —

MAGNESITE
❖ Occurring in white masses, may be cut *en cabochon*
❖ Dyed magnesite often a simulant for TURQUOISE
❖ After being calcined in kilns, used to fabricate firebrick
❖ Also used in manufacturing Epsom salts and face powders

➤ *Magnesite*: Latin, *magnes(ium)*, from Greek, *lithos magnetikos* 'stone from Magnesia (the coastal region of Thessaly)' + *ite* 'rock or part of rock

• Enhances visualization during meditation

MAGNETITE, LODESTONE
❖ Iron oxide, most strongly magnetic naturally occurring mineral on Earth
❖ Magnetic, directional properties known by the ancient Chinese about 2,400 years ago; reported by Marco Polo
❖ Used by Chinese navigators by the 12th Century
❖ Important European navigation aid by the 14th Century, when mentioned by Geoffrey Chaucer in *The Canterbury Tales*
❖ Magnetite crystals found in certain bacteria and in the brains bees, termites, some birds, and humans may relate to *magneto-reception,* the ability to use the Earth's magnetic field in navigation
❖ Important ore of iron
❖ Used as *bluing* to protect steel from rust
❖ Crystallizes a small octahedrons
❖ *Lodestone*: Traditional gemstone for Wednesday

- ➤ *Lodestone*: Middle English, *lode* 'way' + *stone*, from its use as a navigational aid for sailors
- ➤ *Magnetite*: German, *Magnetit, magnet* + *ite* 'rock or part of rock'

- Associated with Water; the planet Venus and the feminine principle; Ares, Capricorn, Aquarius, and Virgo; and the number 4
- Contains the power to repel evil
- Encourages objectivity
- Enables communication with dolphins and whales
- Attracts love and wealth

MALACHITE
- ❖ Brilliant green COPPERderivative, often banded with darker black
- ❖ Frequently found in association with AZURITE
- ❖ Until about 1800, ground to serve as a pigment
- ❖ Soft, measuring 4 on the Mohs scale; usually cut as cabochons or fashioned into beads for jewelry; or carved as ornaments
- ❖ The Malachite Room in The State Hermitage Museum, St. Petersburg, Russia, contains massive ornaments carved from malachite

- ➤ *Malachite*: Greek, *molokhitis* 'mallow-green stone', from *moloche* 'mallow' + *ite* 'rock or mineral'; alternatively, from Greek *malakos*, 'soft', a reference to its softness
- ➤ *Eilat Stone*: Malachite mixed with TURQUOISE and CHRYSOCOLLA

- Associated with Earth and Water; Venus and Neptune; Capricorn, Scorpio, and Pisces; and the number 9
- Ancients: Drinking from malachite vessels made possible communication with animals
- Ancient Egypt: Guards against necromancers and witches when carved with the image of the sun
- Germany: Preserves the wearer from falling

- Italy: Guards against the evil eye (because of the eye-shaped swirls in the stone)
- Powerful healing stone, particularly for healing emotions
- Strengthens teeth, improves eyesight, and warms relationships
- Protects infants, especially when attached to the cradle
- Shatters when danger approaches, thus forewarning the wearer of peril
- When worn or carried, enhances the ability to adjust to change
- Allows insight into the connections between body and mind during illness
- Encourages tolerance of others
- Recently, considered a stone of protection by pilots, air stewards, and others associated with flying
- Green colored in rippled bands exerts a calming effect
- Believed useful in *scrying*, or divination

MARBLE
- ❖ Rock composed of a single mineral, CALCITE
- ❖ Used in signet seals as early as 7,000 B.C.

- ➢ *Marble*: Latin, *marmor,* from Greek, *marmaros* 'marble; originally referring to any hard stone'

- Ancient Greeks: Alchemists wore shards of marble to assist in healing broken bones and injured or diseased skin
- 15th Century Italy: The philosopher Marsilio Ficino taught that an image of the planet Mercury engraved on marble worked against fever (Yates 71)
- Eases anxiety—marble is an excellent "worry stone"

MARCASITE, WHITE IRON PYRITES
- ❖ Associated with Earth and Fire; Venus-Neptune and Taurus; Sun and Leo; Mars-Pluto and Scorpio
- ❖ Chemically similar to PYRITES, but with a different crystal structure

- ❖ Lighter in color and more brittle than PYRITE
- ❖ Soft enough to be scratched with a knife
- ❖ Crystals randomly undergo "pyrite decay," in which they disintegrate into a white powder; the "disease' may even spread to other minerals in a collection
- ❖ In jewelry, most frequently used in *pavé* settings, in which small stones or fragments of stones are place so closely together that none of the backing metal—usually sterling SILVER—shows (although recent analyses suggest that much of the 'marcasite' used in this style of jewelry, particularly during the early 20th century, was in fact a form of pyrite and thus resistant to "pyrite decay')

- ➤ *Marcasite*: Medieval Latin, *marcasita*, ultimately from Arabic/Persian, *marquashita*, 'pyrite'

- • Associated with Water; Moon and Cancer; Mercury and Gemini; Saturn-Uranus and Aquarius
- • New Age: Enhances its wearer's ability to deal with co-dependency

MERCURY, QUICKSILVER, CINNABAR
- ❖ An element as well as a metal; the only metal that is liquid at room temperatures
- ❖ Highly poisonous in its pure substance; a universal solvent (excepting only glass)
- ❖ Considered by some philosophers anciently and during the Renaissance to be one of two essential elements, the second being SULFUR
- ❖ Earlier, considered a key ingredient in medicines and medicinal treatments, often with fatal results; now known to be toxic

- ➤ *Mercury*: Medieval Latin, *Mercurius,* from the Roman god
- ➤ *Quicksilver*: Middle English, *quicksilver*, from Old English *cwicseolfor*, translation of Latin, *argentum vivum—quick* 'living' + silver

- • One of the seven metals associated with Alchemy
- • Symbolizes the planet Mercury

- Alchemically associated with white, with transformation or transmutation, and with purity

MICA, ISINGLASS

❖ Frequently forms as "books," thick accumulations of thin sheet-like crystals

❖ Of the micas, lepidolite is arguably most commonly cut as a gemstone; muscovite books are popular as collectors' specimens

➤ *Mica*: New Latin, *micere* 'to shine'; from Latin, *mica* 'grain'

➤ *Biotite, Iron Mica*: German, *Biotit*, named after Jean-Baptiste *Biot* + *ite* 'rock or mineral'; dark brown or black

➤ *Clintonite*: Named for De Witt *Clinton* + *ite* 'rock or mineral'; brittle, ranges from colorless to yellow, green, red, brown

➤ *Glauconite*: Greek, *glaucos* 'gleaming, silvery' + *ite* 'rock of mineral'; describing the blue-green color; used as a green pigment ("terre verte" or "green earth"), particularly in Russian icons

➤ *Fuchsite*: shimmering green variety of muscovite

➤ *Isinglass*: Middle Dutch, *huysenblase* 'sturgeon's bladder', from the resemblance of this sheets of transparent mica to a gelatin, used in glue and jellies, prepared from the bladder of sturgeons; earlier used as a window material for furnaces

➤ *Lepidolite*: Latin: lepido 'scale' + *ite* 'rock or mineral'; lilac or rose-colored

➤ *Margarite*: Middle English, *margarite* 'pearl'; ultimately from Iranian/Pahlavi *marvarit* 'pearl'; brittle, white to pinkish or yellow-grey

➤ *Muscovite, White Mica*: From *Muscovy*-glass + *ite* 'rock or mineral', formerly used as windows in Russia; colorless (occasionally red, yellow, green, brown, or grey); also called *cat's silver*

➤ *Paragonite, Natron-Glimmer*: Greek, *paragon* 'misleading' + *ite* 'rock or mineral'; colorless or pale brown

➤ *Phlogopite*: Greek, phlogopos 'fiery-looking' + ite 'rock or mineral'; yellow, green or reddish-brown, similar to biotite; used in insulation

➤ *Zinnwaldite*: Named for *Zinnwald*, Germany + *ite* 'Rock or mineral'; yellow-brown mica, found in association with tin ores

- Protects its wearer against earthquakes

MILKY QUARTZ
❖ Among the most common materials found on the Earth's surface
❖ Variably opaque variety of QUARTZ, often showing milky bands caused by gasses and liquids trapped in the crystal
❖ Rarely cut as a gemstone, but used for beads and ornaments
❖ Crystal frequently large, including one from Siberia weighing over 14.5 tons

MOISSONITE
❖ Contemporary DIAMOND simulant, available commercially since the late 1990s
❖ Gem-quality silicon carbide available only from C3 Inc
❖ Even though lab-created, stones may run in excess of $500 per carat

MOLDAVITE
❖ A TEKTITE, or gemstone formed from a meteor; hence, moldavite is extraterrestrial
❖ Formed about 20,000,000 years ago during a meteor shower in the former Czechoslovakia
❖ Possibly formed in outer space; more likely the result of materials from the meteors melting and fusing with other elements

➢ *Moldavite:* From *Moldau* Valley, site of the original meteor impact + *ite* 'rock or mineral'

- Facilitates personal growth; allows wearers to release everything that holds them to old ideas

MOONSTONE, ADULARIA MOONSTONE
❖ Most valuable of the FELDSPAR group; adularia FELDSPAR with a white shimmer
❖ Found in India and Australia
❖ White or yellowish stone, characterized by a blue or white *schiller, opalescence, adularescence,* or flash, caused by internal

parallel layers of albite and orthoclase FELDSPAR

❖ Cut as cabochons or beads

➢ *Adularia*: French, *adulaire*, named after *Adula,* a mountain in Switzerland

- Associated with Water; Moon; Venus and Neptune; Cancer, Libra, Scorpio, and Pisces; and the number 4
- Anciently: Associated with the Moon, which rules the night; hence a magical talisman of unusual power
- Ancient India: Considered a sacred stone—usually displayed against a yellow background since yellow is a sacred color
- Ancient India: If lovers place a bit of moonstone in their mouths during the full moon, they can foretell the future
- Ancient Orient: A good luck stone
- 11th Century Europe: Brings about lovers' reconciliations—popular gift for lovers
- 16th Century: Eliminates insomnia
- Traditionally a 'Traveler's Stone,' protecting merchants and traders while at sea
- Associated with witchcraft (white) and goddess-worship
- Protects its wearer from evil magic
- Reflects mood changes
- Enhances propensity for prophetic dreaming
- Aids in meditation
- Arouses and intensifies feelings of warmth and friendship when passed between lovers
- Marks the waxing and waning of the moon; its color brightens as the beginning of each new moon
- Talisman of good fortune
- *Peach Moonstone*: A naturally occurring form with a warm, peach tone
- *Rainbow Moonstone*: A naturally occurring form with translucent blue highlights

- *Silver Moonstone*: A naturally occurring form in silver-grey

MORGANITE
- ❖ Pink variety of BERYL
- ❖ First discovered at the beginning of the 20th Century in Pala, California
- ❖ Dichroic, showing pink and blush-pink
- ❖ When heat-treated, become blue

- ➢ *Morganite*: Named for financier and gemstone collector J. P. *Morgan* + *ite* 'rock or mineral', in 1911 by G. F. Kunz, chief collector for Tiffany & company

MOSS AGATE
- ❖ CHALCEDONY variant colored with tendrils or 'dendrites' of intrusive minerals, usually oxides. The branch-like or fern-like appearance of the inclusions provides the name.

- Associated with Taurus
- Augments positive emotions
- Bestows a 'green thumb' upon its wearer; allows the wearer to perceive the beauty of Nature
- Heals the pain of a stiff neck
- Assists in finding lost/hidden treasure

MOSS AGATE

And thus the Grene Knyht sports with Arthur's band,
Transience meets immortality—
Sir Gawain strikes the blow, beheads the Man…

As I behead last summer's stiff-mown weeds
Bold-grown and proud—ruff-necked, haut, gaudy for
My fatal stroke. Rude act—rude play, perhaps—
But necessary (as I think)—green gore
To pay for Fall's regenerative lapse—
Yet from the crystal-sharded rime of snow
Dendritic aches to full contractions swell
Seeded by the frozen-garnet glow

That with my hasty sword-stroke, dying, fell—

Molecule upon molecule tissue-flesh
Rebuilds, rises into spring breezes fresh

MOTHER-OF-PEARL, SEE ABALONE

— N —

NEVADA LAPIS, LAPIS NEVADA, NEVADA JADE, ATLAS STONE

* ❖ Discovered in the mid-1950s and first made public as a semi-precious gemstone in 1989
* ❖ Variety of CHALCEDONY, colored by inclusions of THULITE (light pink ZOISITE); DIOPSIDE (moss green, gray-green); and MICROCLINE, as well as at least seven other minerals in combination
* ❖ Scientific name: thulite-diopside skarn, *skarn* being the common term for a rock formed by metamorphosis of granite—in this case a granite some 170 million years old. Skarn is found throughout the world, but this combination of colors and gemstone quality is rare
* ❖ In spite of its name, Nevada Lapis is not related to *Lapis Lazuli*
* ❖ Occasionally (but inaccurately) called 'Pink Unakite'

* ➢ *Nevada:* Spanish, *Nevada* 'snowy, snowfall' + Greek, *lapis,* 'rock, stone'

* • Associated with Taurus and Gemini
* • Helps the wearer become aware of and control integral healing powers, especially when applying them to others
* • Enhances protection and promotes courage
* • Helps bring male and female energies into balance
* • Acts as a source of creativity
* • *Atlas Stone*: alleviates the carrying of heavy burdens

— O —

OBSIDIAN

❖ Naturally formed volcanic glass, formed by lava cooling so rapidly that no crystals can form in it

❖ Usually dark grey to black, due to the presence of iron or magnesium, although translucent in thin flakes

❖ In chemical composition, similar to granite

❖ Not a true mineral, since there are no crystals; instead, is referred to as a *mineraloid*

❖ Used by primitive cultures for knives, arrowheads, spearheads, sword blades mounted in wood, and other weapons; the oldest examples are more than 25,000 years old

❖ Used in constructing the gigantic Easter Island sculptures called *Moai*

❖ Contemporary uses include specialized blades for cardiac surgery, since the obsidian can be many times sharper than surgical steel

➢ *Obsidian*: 14th C. Latin, *Obsidianus,* a printer's error for *Obsianus*, referring to *Obsius*, according to the historian Pliny the discoverer of a stone—*Obsius lapis*—that resembled contemporary Obsidian

➢ *Apache Tears*: Small nodules of grey-to-black obsidian

➢ *Gold-sheen Obsidian*: Displays a distinct gold sheen, caused by included minerals or elongated, reflecting gas bubbles in the structure of the natural glass

➢ *Green-sheen Obsidian*: Similar patterning of included minerals or captured gas bubbles, resulting in a greenish reflection

➢ *Mahogany Obsidian*: Characteristically dark obsidian streaked with a red-to-brown pattern suggesting mahogany

➢ *Rainbow Obsidian*: Captured gas bubbles or included minerals

- ➤ *Silver-sheen Obsidian*: Similar included minerals or bubbles result in deep silver iridescent banding
- ➤ *Snowflake Obsidian*: Black matrix included with small irregular clusters of white-to-grey cristobalite
- ➤ Other varieties include: *Brown, Green, Flame, Lizard Skin, Midnight Lace, Pumpkin, Red,* and others

- Associated with Earth and Fire; Saturn; Mars and Pluto, God of the Underworld
- Ancient Aztecs: Obsidian considered a warrior's stone; obsidian used to form images of the god Tezcatlipoca (also known as "Smoking Mirror"); obsidian mirrors facilitate divination
- Since black opposes light, black obsidian lends the wearer invisibility
- 16th Century England: John Dee, mathematician and astrologer to Queen Elizabeth I, used obsidian as a scrying stone
- New Age: Aids in making decisions
- New Age: Enhances the courage to stand by one's convictions
- New Age: Facilitates meditation to overcome fears or barriers
- New Age: Works to inhibit depression
- *Black Obsidian*: Aids in divination by providing a highly polished surface into which one might gaze; enhances libido and harmonizes relationships between men and women; helps remove residual psychic energies trapped within the physical body
- *Brown Obsidian*: Releases fears that otherwise would hold one back
- *Gold-sheen Obsidian*: Encourages the wearer to "go for the gold"; enhances one's ability to penetrate to the root of a problem
- *Green-sheen Obsidian*: Brings its wearer wealth and health; helps alleviate jet-lag and nightmares
- *Grey/Silver Obsidian*: Aids in spirit-travel; assists in shamanic rituals

- *Mahogany Obsidian*: enhances physical strength and helps in achieving goals; helps to overcome inherited or cultural beliefs that inhibit full development
- *Midnight Lace Obsidian*: Harmonizes light and darkness; helps the wearer to overcome the temptation to either/or conclusions
- *Rainbow Obsidian*: Brings its wearer love, joy, and light
- *Red Obsidian*: Assists the libido and harmonizes relationships between men and women; helps to overcome childhood traumas
- *Snowflake Obsidian*: Helps bring awareness of light into the darkness

OBSIDIAN TURTLE

Obsidian turtle
Crawls from solid earth to sky—
Soul in sculpted sand....

AZTEC

A splendor of spears
vibrates the dusky plains

obsidian blows shudder
the hexagon of death

muted blood-lust
and captive-tallies stand complete

gods appeasable
and famine surfeited in blood-to-be

Smoking Mirror
Southern Hummingbird
gullets and maws
too long empty

in six directions swirls
the splendor of spears—six armies

chanting homeward
from the Flower Battle

to feed emaciated manifestations
of the god

atop pyramids, and wait pregnantly
for sky-casks to burst.

THE VISION OF MOCTEZUMA

Moctezuma told the Elders of his vision,
Black obsidian vision bird-borne
As the grey bird flew into the Council Room.

A grey bird—cold-colored as dew in a storm-time
Dawning—fluttering among the vibrant colors
Ornamenting the Elders' shrunken arms;

And on its forehead, a mirror
Of polished obsidian. Among those present,
Moctezuma alone perceived in the mirror

All the Stars of the Universe.
And as he watched
They changed—

And in their places stood strange shining warriors,
Metal-clad, who reached and grasped
And wrenched familiar shapes

Into strangeness. As the stars
Died, screams of pain
Wreathed about the heads of dying gods.

This Moctezuma told his Elders
As he became one with the mirror
Glowing in the forehead of Texcatlipoca's messenger.

ODONTOLITE [SEE TURQUOISE]
OLIVINE [SEE PERIDOT]

ONYX [SEE ALSO CHALCEDONY]

❖ Frequently characterized by parallel layers of color, Onyx is particularly valued for use in cameos and intaglios

❖ Differs from AGATE only in that the colored bands are parallel and more regular

❖ Black Onyx is usually dyed to ensure consistent color

❖ Usually cut into cabochons or beads, often in directions that accentuate the natural banding

❖ Traditional birthstone for the sign Virgo and for Capricorn

❖ Traditional birthstone for July

➤ *Onyx*: Middle English, *onix*, ultimately from the Greek, *onux,* 'claw,' 'fingernail'—referring to the occasional streak of pink within white, resembling the lunula of a fingernail

• Ancient Rome: Provides protection during nocturnal journeys and in battle; enhances sense of calm; decreases lust

• Ancient India: Provided protection against the evil eye

• Ancient Middle East: Acted as a worry stone to absorb negative energy

• Strengthens the ability to concentrate; helps overcome apathy

• Contains strong protective powers; carried into battle, protects warriors

• Eliminates negative thinking

• *Black Onyx*: Ameliorates grief and enhances self-control

• *Pale Green Onyx*: enhances emotional balance and calm

ONYX

Onyx
Is Jupiter,
King of Worlds – rust-ground Sphere
He glowers lesser Gods with His
Great Eye

OPAL

❖ Three basic forms: *precious* or opalescent opal; yellow-red transparent *fire* opal; non-opalescent *common* opal

❖ Non-crystalline, amorphous, solid gel variety of QUARTZ prized for its play of color but that otherwise displays almost none of the traditional qualities of gemstones—it is usually opaque rather than transparent, soft, fragile, susceptible to dehydration and *crazing*, breaks easily, lacks durability, and is difficult if not impossible to facet

❖ Pure opal is colorless, but almost all varieties contain impurities that result in a wide spectrum of colors, red being the most prized

❖ Prized second only to EMERALD by the ancient Romans

❖ Set in the Crown Jewels of France

❖ Australian legend has the cosmos controlled by an immense opal that controls gold and human love; the Aborigines tell of OPAL as a human-serpent devil lying in wait to destroy humans with flashes of evil fire; in another variant of the tale, the Storm God, in a fit of jealousy against beauty, shattered the Rainbow, and the fragments became opals

❖ Most opal is more than 60,000,000 years old, dating from the age of dinosaurs

❖ Because of its unique play of colors—called *opalescence*— opal remains among the most highly prized of all gemstones

❖ *Black Opal* first discovered in Australia in 1887

❖ *White Opal* discovered in Australia in 1889

❖ Traditional birthstone for October and for the 13th wedding anniversary; alternatively, for the 14th and 18th anniversaries

➤ *Opal*: Sanskrit, *upala*, and Latin, *opalus,* both meaning 'precious stone'

➤ *Agate Opal*: Agate showing light and dark layers of opal

➤ *Black Opal*: Precious opal with a dark (but not black) background, which highlights the flashes of fire

➤ *Boulder Opal*: Precious opal from Queensland, Australia, that has formed as a very thin layer on a matrix rock of dark iron-stone; the finest specimens may demand up to $1,000 per carat

➢ *Bubble Opal*: a satin flash hyalite opal exhibiting a distinctive *adularescence* (or milky luster) from small bubble-like structures within the stone; found in gem-quality only in Utah; in its rough state, known as *Bacon-rind Rock* for its layers of clear-to-white, cream, and purple; or *Milford Opal* for the town of Milford, Utah, near its source

➢ *Common Opal*: Material with the same composition as precious opal but lacking any *opalescence*; in spite of the term *common*, such opal exhibits beautiful colors—including pink and blue—and is itself prized by collectors and jewelers

➢ *Crystal Opal*: Transparent variety that exhibits flacks of red opalescence on its surface rather than from within

➢ *Doublet*: A thin layer of precious opal mounted on a dark-to-black surface, such as OBSIDIAN, ONYX, glass or plastic

➢ *Fire Opal*: Usually transparent opal with intense red, yellow, or orange body color but no fire, frequently found small blebs in RHYOLITE; one of the few varieties that is faceted rather than cut *en cabochon*; most comes from Mexico

➢ *Gilson Opal*: A synthetic material named for Pierre *Gilson*, Sr., who developed the technique to create stones that mimic all of the properties of natural opal except for their water content

➢ *Girasol*: Italian, *girasole* 'sunflower, opal'; nearly colorless, transparent opal with a faint bluish bluster

➢ *Harlequin Opal*: a rare variety in which a vivid play of color occurs in regular squares or rectangles

➢ *Honey Opal*: Yellow translucent opal, named for its resemblance to honey

➢ *Hyalite, Glass Opal*: A clear, colorless, glass-like jelly OPAL, named from Greek, *hualos* 'glass' + *ite* 'rock or mineral'

➢ *Hydrophane*: A variety that is opaque when dry and nearly transparent when wet

➢ *Jelly Opal*: Usually transparent opal so called because it looks like a blob of jelly caught within the matrix rock

➢ *Milk Opal*: White, opaque common opal

- ➤ *Moss Opal*: White, opaque dendritic milk opal
- ➤ *Opaline, Opal Matrix*: Banded or leafed inclusion of precious opal into a matrix rock
- ➤ *Opalized Wood, Wood Opal*: PETRIFIED WOOD in which organic materials have been replaced by opal
- ➤ *Porcelain Opal*: White, opaque common opal
- ➤ *Prase Opal*: Apple-green opal that resembles chrysoprase
- ➤ *Precious Opal*: Opal displaying the characteristic opalescence, or plays of color
- ➤ *Precious Fire Opal*: Fire opal that exhibits the characteristic opalescence
- ➤ *Seam Opal*: Precious opal that has formed in seams or cracks in rocks
- ➤ *Spencer Opal*: Precious and common opal from a privately owned mine near Spencer, Idaho
- ➤ *Triplet*: A doublet covered by a thin protective layer of transparent QUARTZ, glass, or hard plastic
- ➤ *Wax Opal*: Yellow-brown opal with a waxy luster
- ➤ *White Opal*: Precious opal with a light or white background
- ➤ *Yowah Nuts*: Rounded nodules of boulder opal found in the Yowah area of Queensland, with flashes of fire embedded in ironstone matrix

- • Associated with Air; with all planets and Zodiac signs
- • Australian Aborigines: Functions as a gateway to 'dreamtime' and to visions
- • Ancients: Aids its wearer to attain invisibility and to travel by spirit (astral projection)—thus the stone became a talisman for thieves or spies
- • Ancients: Symbol of faithfulness and confidence
- • Greeks: Provides the wearer with the gift of prophecy
- • Romans: Ensures the wearer love and hope
- • Arabs: The stone fell from heaven, accompanied by a burst of lightning
- • Middle-Ages: Referred to as the "eye-stone"; thought to have

formed from children's eyes

- Middle-Ages: Considered a cure for all eye diseases
- 14th Century Venice: Became brilliant when the owner contracted the Black Plague, then faded when the owner died—hence one source of the reputation of opal as a bad-luck stone
- 17th Century France: Louis XIV named his coaches after gemstones; since the driver of the *Opal* was frequently drunk, the stone's reputation for ill-luck was enhanced.
- "Bad Luck Stone": May only safely be worn by a Libra or Scorpio (October birthday), whose birthstone it is. One source for this tradition may lie in Sir Walter Scott's novel *Anne of Geierstein*, in which a character dies after holy water quenches the fire in her magic OPAL (Sofianides and Harlow 122; Elsbeth 176). An alternate suggestion is that, during a surge in popularity of the stone during the early 19th century, jewelers began circulating rumors of the stone's bad luck, since opals are notoriously fragile and if a stone fractured while being set, the jeweler was held responsible for the cost; in essence the tradition might have been a kind of self-protection for the jewelers
- New Age: Magnifies hidden strengths or weaknesses of the wearer; psychically neutral
- Cures eye diseases and renders the wearer invisible
- Considered a living stone that can move forward in time
- Essentially a feminine stone
- Efficacious in lightening the pains of childbirth
- Works to counter emerging grey hairs in blonde women
- Do not play well with others; opals should be kept away from other gemstones
- *Black Opal*: Lucky stone, particularly when mounted in GOLD and worn near the heart
- *Black Opal*: Protects travelers on long journeys
- *Black Opal*: Effects the reproductive organs, spleen, and pancreas
- *Black Opal*: Alleviates depression, especially sexually related

- *Common opal*: Enhances the wearer's self-esteem, thereby simultaneously attracting wealth, love, peace
- *Fire Opal*: Works on red corpuscle to alleviate blood disorders, depression, apathy, lethargy
- *White Opal*: Balances left and right brain

ROMAN OMEN

For Miss Miles and her "Opal"

Josephine
speaks its evil

moans its milk-bright
white
and screens
its fortune-haunted greens
and reds
embedded

in cold death-pale
lattice opal.

OPALITE[1] [SEE BERTRANDITE]

OPALITE[2]

- ❖ Although not a naturally occurring gemstone, Opalite, a form of glass made in China, is increasingly available, often under names that suggest natural gemstones
- ❖ To indicate that the material is not naturally occurring, the names often include strategic quotation marks, as in Opalized "Quartz" or Sea "Opal"
- ❖ Opalite is cut, polished, and faceted into jewelry, cabochons, and beads

- ➢ *Opalite*: Named for its iridescent sheen, suggestive of natural *Opal* + *ite* 'rock or mineral'
- ➢ Varieties include Chalcedony Opalite, Moonstone Quartz, Opalized Quartz, Ruby Opalite, Sea Opal, and others

ORTHOCLASE, POTASH FELDSPAR

- ❖ Massive orthoclase a primary constituent of granite
- ❖ Transparent, colorless variety of FELDSPAR, cut primarily as a collectors' gemstone
- ❖ Found in a single location in Madagascar
- ❖ When cut *en cabochon*, displays *chatoyancy*

- ➢ *Orthoclase*: Greek, *ortho* 'straight' + *clase*, from Greek *klasis* 'cleavage, breaking'

— P —

PAUA SHELL, SEE ALSO ABALONE

❖ New Zealand variety of Abalone shell, distinctive for its unusually vivid pinks, reds, purples, and blues

❖ Brilliant iridescence, similar to that in OPAL, makes it valuable in jewelry

❖ Dark veins are formed by layers of proteins between parallel layers of calcium

❖ Traditionally, the Maori retain the right to harvest Paua, which is edible, regardless of other legal restrictions

➤ *Paua*: Maori, *paua* 'abalone'

• Originally prized by the Maori, who used it for the eyes of carvings; the red tones symbolized a warrior's strength and passion

• Clears the body of stressful hormones

PEACOCK COPPER, PEACOCK ORE [SEE BORNITE]

PEARL

❖ One of the few organic gemstones (along with CORAL, IVORY, AMBER, and JET)

❖ Composed primarily of microscopic layers of ARAGONITE or CALCITE, deposited around a foreign object; the developed pearl is essentially a protective device to avoid irritation

❖ Birthstone for the sign Cancer

❖ Traditional gemstone for Monday

➤ *Pearl*: Middle English, *perle,* ultimately from Latin, *perna,* 'ham' or 'sea-mussel'—referring to the ham-shape of the shell

- ➤ *Baroque Pearl*: Irregularly shaped pearls; during the Renaissance much sought after as a basis for highly imaginative GOLD- and SILVER-work
- ➤ *Blister Pearl*: Incompletely formed pearl, still attached to the shell
- ➤ *Margarita*: Latin word for Pearl
- ➤ *Tahitian Black Pearl*: In generally, the most valuable form of pearl
- ➤ *Wai Momi*: Hawaiian, "pearl waters" or Pearl Harbor

- Associated with Water; Moon; Cancer/Scorpio/Pisces
- Indian mythology: Considered "heavenly dewdrops that fell into the sea and were caught by shellfish under the first rays of the rising sun during a period of full moon" (Sofianides and Harlow 176)—the belief was later adopted by Europeans
- Hebrew mythology: Derive from Eve's tears when she was expelled from Eden
- Ancient China: Assures wealth, honor, and long life
- 16th Century Europe: Queen Elizabeth I was so enamored with Pearls, and their associations with purity and virginity, that she frequently had them sewn onto her gowns; one such gown contained over 500,000 pearls[1]
- 17th Century Europe: Pearls still considered effective medicine

---

[1] An additional element to the Queen's fascination with pearls stemmed from their inherent value as portable signifiers of wealth. Tradition has it that Elizabeth gave orders that the pearls adorning her State Gowns be sewn on so loosely that when she walked, the sheer weight and number of pearls would cause some to break loose, fall, and roll across the floor. As a mark of her wealth and stature as Queen of England, Elizabeth would ignore them. The tradition continues, however, to note that Elizabeth, a notoriously thrifty monarch, would nevertheless detail servants to make certain that all of her pearls were recovered.

Elizabeth's successor, James I, perhaps valued them less highly, but his wife and consort, Anne of Denmark, nearly matched Elizabeth's obsession with pearls. For one of the masques written for Queen Anne by Ben Jonson, the costume designs for Anne and her Ladies required so many pearls that one journalist noted, in a rather awed tone, that there was not a pearl to be purchased anywhere in the City of London.

for a variety of ailments, especially when ground or dissolved

- Associated with femininity
- Associated with love; hence particularly appropriate as orna-mentation at weddings
- When worn, purify the blood and regulate biorhythms
- Provides a soothing influence
- Symbolizes wisdom and purity
- Symbolizes that which is precious, as in "Pearls of wisdom," or "Pearl of great price"
- Strongly magical properties work despite the fact that harvesting pearls requires the death of its host-animal

PEARL PARINGS

Pearl parings on
    apricot tapestry; new
        moon arcs at sunset

PERIDOT, OLIVINE, CHRYSOLITE

- ❖ Name for a variety of green, transparent OLIVINE
- ❖ Anciently, mined for nearly 3,000 years almost exclusively on a desolate island—Zabargad or Zebirget (now St. John's Island)—in the Red Sea
- ❖ Earliest sources: Egypt, peridot beads, circa 1580-1350 B.C.
- ❖ Greece and Rome: 3rd and 4th Centuries B.C.
- ❖ Brought to Europe by the Crusaders during the Middle Ages
- ❖ Most popular stone during the Baroque period (late Renaissance)
- ❖ Largely rediscovered in the early 20th Century
- ❖ One of the few gemstones that occurs in a single color, although its characteristic green may be lighter or darker, depending on internal structures
- ❖ Relatively rare, primarily found in small crystals, although the largest faceted peridot, in the Smithsonian Museum, Washing-ton, D.C., weighs 310 carats

- ❖ Less popular than many gemstones, largely from its lack of luster and tendency to cleave easily
- ❖ Some Russian peridot were cut from material that fell in a meteorite in Siberia in 1749
- ❖ Traditional gemstone for Libra
- ❖ Traditional birthstone for August

- ➢ *Chrysolite*: Greek, *chrysolithos*, from *chryso-* 'gold' + *lithos* 'stone'—alternate name for a yellow variety of peridot; originally applied to other similarly colored stones as well
- ➢ *Olivine* German, *Olivin*, olive + *ine*, from its distinctive color,
- ➢ *Peridot*: Arabic, *faridat* 'gem'; alternatively French, *peritot*, 'unclear'
- ➢ *Zabargad*: Arabic, 'olivine'

- • Associated with Earth and Fire; Venus and Taurus; Sun and Leo; Mars-Pluto and Scorpio
- • Anciently through the Middle Ages: Symbolizes the sun; endows its owner with almost royal dignity
- • Middle Ages: Used to predict the future when incised with the image of a mule
- • Protects wearers from evil spirits—but only when pierces, strung on the hair of a donkey, then tied around the owner's left arm
- • Invites wealth, especially when engraved with a torchbearer, the symbol of the sun
- • Associated with healing with expelling negative emotions
- • Traditionally diminishes anger and lessens jealousy
- • Transmitter of healing energies
- • Opens life to enlargement and adventure

PETERSITE [SEE PIETERSITE]

PETRIFIED WOOD
- ❖ FOSSILIZED wood, in which all organic materials have been replaced, usually with a silicon-based substance such as QUARTZ
- ❖ Frequently the internal organic structures, including veining and

tree-rings, are still visible
- ❖ Some nearly intact petrified trees reach a length of 100 feet
- ❖ Pure QUARTZ is colorless, but petrified wood frequently occurs—and is valued in jewelry and as collectors' specimens—for the variety of colors caused by associated minerals, such as:

> CARBON: black
> COBALT: blue and green
> CHROMIUM: blue and green
> COPPER: blue and green
> IRON OXIDES: red, brown, yellow
> MANGANESE: pink and orange
> MANGANESE OXIDES: black

- ❖ In some instances, specifically in Australia, petrified wood has *opalized*
- ❖ As a semi-precious gemstone, quite hard, 7 on the Mohs scale (as is QUARTZ)
- ❖ Curiously enough, scientists in Washington recently created a lab-grown/artificial tungsten carbide petrified wood
- ❖ State gem of Washington
- ❖ Petrified *Palmwood* is the state stone of Texas and the state fossil of Louisiana
- ❖ Official provincial stone of Alberta, Canada

- ➤ *Petrified*: Latin and Greek, *petra* 'stone' + *facere* 'to make'
- ➤ Varieties considered semi-precious gemstones include: *Bog Wood, Bog Palm, Palmwood*

- • Associated with Earth; Saturn; Taurus, Virgo, Capricorn
- • Considered the Earth's record-keeper
- • Brings its wearer all of the benefits of AGATE
- • Aids longevity (as do other sorts of fossils)
- • Protects its wearer from drowning
- • Aids in astral projection when a piece is placed on the small of the back

PHENAKITE, PHENACITE
❖ Gem-quality transparent crystals occasionally cut as gemstones
❖ Generally bears a visual resemblance to QUARTZ crystals
❖ Faceted crystals are brilliant enough to be occasionally mistaken for DIAMOND
❖ Faceted specimens as large as 43 carats are known

➤ *Phenakite*: Greek, *phenak* 'imposter' + *ite* 'rock or mineral'

PIETERSITE, PETERSITE
❖ Thus far discovered in only two locations: China and Africa, with the two varieties sharing similarities but clearly distinct in color and internal composition
❖ Chinese pietersite only discovered a decade ago
❖ Both varieties contain brecciated (fragmented, broken) fibrous bands of red, blue, or gold TIGER'S EYE embedded in QUARTZ
❖ The process of fracturing and reformation results in spectacular colors and *chatoyancy*

➤ *Pietersite*: Named after its discoverer, Sid *Pieters* + *ite* 'rock or mineral'; first located in Namibia, Africa, in 1962

• Blue Pietersite enhances the wearer's ability to teach and communicate

PLASMA
❖ Opaque green form of CHALCEDONY, colored by various silicates
❖ Most commonly found in semi-precious gemstones as the green component of BLOODSTONE

➤ *Plasma*: Greek, *plasma* 'something molded or formed', from Greek, *plassein* 'to mold'

PLATINUM
❖ First noted as a gem-quality precious metal in 1735, at a mine in Colombia, South America
❖ Platinum does not tarnish, but has a faint bluish tinge when compared with SILVER
❖ Associated with Water; Neptune and Pisces; compatible with all

crystals, gems, minerals

❖ Since 1971, also refers to a recording that has sold over a million copies, hence, unusually valuable

➤ *Platinum*: Spanish, *platina*, from *plat* 'silver-like' + *ina* 'made of or resembling'

PRASE, EMERALD QUARTZ

❖ Transparent green form of CHALCEDONY, colored by chlorite inclusions
❖ Greece: Used as a gemstone circa 400 B.C.

➤ *Prase*: Greek, *prase,* 'leek; hence, green'

PRASIOLITE, VERMARINE

❖ Not usually a naturally occurring form of QUARTZ; results from heat-treating AMETHYST or yellowish QUARTZ from a specific deposit in Brail
❖ Naturally occurring prasiolite reported in a mine in Poland
❖ Available only since 1950
❖ Leek-green, although the color may fade in sunlight

➤ *Prasiolite*: Greek, *prason,* 'leek' + *ite* 'rock or mineral'

PREHNITE

❖ Identified as a separate mineral species in 1788
❖ Gem-quality samples may display distinct *chatoyancy* (cat's-eye effect) or *pleochroism* (show different colors when viewed from different directions)
❖ Usually occurs massively rather than as distinct crystals
❖ Usually cut *en cabochon*, but occasionally faceted
❖ When tumbled with part of its matrix still attached, presents a striking contrast of clear green and deep brown

➤ *Prehnite*: Named after its discoverer, Colonel Hendrick von *Prehn* + *ite* 'rock or mineral'; first discovered at the Cape of Good Hope, South Africa; the first mineral to be named after a person
➤ *Cape Emerald*: Earlier trade name for gem-quality varieties

- Has a calming effect, as a result of its soft green color

PYRITE, IRON PYRITES

❖ Notorious as "Fool's Gold," so-called because its metallic luster imitates the more precious metal; paradoxically, it is often associated in nature with true GOLD

❖ Has the same chemical formula as MARCASITE, also known as White Iron Pyrites or Spear Pyrites

❖ One of the Earth's most common minerals

❖ Naturally occurs in clusters of nearly perfect cubes, often with striated faces; larger clusters are valuable as collectors' specimens

❖ Crystals may reach nearly 8 inches across

❖ Occurs as small embedded crystals—and adds flash and color—to LAPIS LAZULI and various forms of JASPER

❖ During World War II, mined as a source of SULFUR to produce sulfuric acid

➢ *Pyrite*: Latin *pyrites,* 'flint,' 'pyrite'; from Greek *purites* 'of fire', *pur* or *pyr*, 'fire' + *ite* 'rock or mineral'—hence, 'firestone'

➢ *Pyrites*: Also refers to any metallic sulfides that spark when struck with steel

- Associated with Air; Mercury and Gemini; Moon and Cancer; Saturn-Uranus and Aquarius

- Associated with Leo and the number 3

- North American Indians: Aids in divination and healing

- Mesoamerican cultures: Aids in scrying when formed into mirrors (see also Obsidian mirrors)

- Brings the wearer good luck and wealth

- Stone of protection

— Q —

QUARTZ

- ❖ Varieties of Quartz include such diverse semi-precious gem-stones as ACTINOLATED QUARTZ, AGATE, AMETHYST, AVEN-TURINE, BLOODSTONE, BLUE QUARTZ, CARNELIAN, CAT'S EYE QUARTZ, CHALCEDONY, CHERT, CITRINE, FLINT, JASPER, MILKY QUARTZ, OPAL, ROCK CRYSTAL, ROSE QUARTZ, RUTILATED QUARTZ, SMOKY QUARTZ, TIGER'S EYE QUARTZ, TOURMALI-NATED QUARTZ, and others
- ❖ Earliest sources—ROCK CRYSTAL: Associated with prehistoric cultures, circa 75,000 B.C.
- ❖ Earliest sources—AMETHYST, ornamental: France, neolithic cultures, circa 25,000 B.C.
- ❖ Near East: ROCK CRYSTAL seal-cylinders, circa 4,000 B.C.
- ❖ Egypt: Amulets and gems, circa 3,100 B.C.
- ❖ Hebrews: AMETHYST formed the 9th stone in the Breastplate of the High Priest
- ❖ Among the commonest of minerals; second most common rock-forming mineral
- ❖ Composed of nearly pure silica
- ❖ Occurs in massive microcrystalline forms (as AGATE, BLOODSTONE, CHALCEDONY, JASPER, etc.) and crystalline forms (as ROCK CRYSTAL, AMETHYST, CITRINE, etc.)
- ❖ Used to control the frequency of radio transmitters; hence, the earlier forms of "crystal" radios
- ❖ Crystals may show a number of variations, including:
  Clusters: Multiple individual crystals spreading outward from a common matrix
  Enhydro Crystals: Contains a water pocket within the crystal
  Herkimer Diamonds: Double-terminated crystals formed in small pockets within the matrix material

> *Phantom Crystals*: Containing ghost-like or phantom images of themselves inside the structure
>
> *Scepters*: Crystals composed of a larger termination on a smaller stalk or stem, resembling a monarch's scepter

- ➢ *Quartz*: German, *Quarz*, from Middle High German, *quarc* or *twarc*, from Slavic, *kwardy*, 'hard' (Czech, *tvrdy*; Polish, *twardy*); Latinized version first recorded in the 16th Century
- ➢ *Crystal*: Greek, *krystallos*, 'ice', from the earlier *kryos*, 'icy cold'—The ancient Greeks believed crystals (especially colorless quartz crystals) to be ice by the gods so completely as to remain so forever
- ➢ *Cairngorm*: Scottish, name given to Smoky Quartz from their source in the Cairngorm Mountains
- ➢ *Rainbow Quartz, Iris Quartz*: Rock crystal showing internal cracks, or *veils*, which produce a play of color when light stricks thin films of air within the cracks

- Associated with Fire and Air; Sagittarius; Mercury and Virgo
- Aids in divination and scrying when formed into a clear ball
- Carries healing properties
- Used in shamanic healing and other rituals because of their ability to increase and strengthen an individual's aura; often considered a living being that required 'feeding' by rubbing it with blood
- *Rock Crystal*: Ancient Japanese considered it the perfect jewel, symbolizing purity, clarity, infinity, patience, and perseverance
- *Rock Crystal*; Fashioned into a ball, enhances the owner's magical powers, enables the owner to foresee the future, to cure diseased cattle, etc.
- *Asterated quartz/Cat's eye quartz*: Brings hope and inspiration

QUARTZITE

- ❖ Originally sandstone, then altered by heat and pressure, quartzite may consist of as much as 90% pure microcrystalline QUARTZ in a tightly interlocking matrix
- ❖ Extremely hard at 7 on the Mohs scale

- ❖ Included minerals may color it blue, green, purple, or black
- ❖ Because of its hardness, takes and retains a high polish, making it useful when cut *en cabochon*

- ➢ *Quartzite*: From *quartz* + *ite* 'rock or mineral'; distinctively hard, massive rock formed of microscopic Quartz crystals
- ➢ *Quartzite*: Town in Arizona, named for nearby deposits of Quartzite, that has become an important trading center for rocks, minerals, and semi-precious gemstones

QUARTZITE SANDSTONE

—sand-and-banded-stone mottled-blood-
engorged-forging-thrusting-skyward pinnacle
mud-and-blood-pressured-stone tower cold-
ly wearing iron weight of years nipping

wind-tears cracking pins of elemental
ice burst infinitesimal fractures wedge submicroscopic molecules—
moisture waging immortal war with mock-

ing grit […] scouring wind […] blistering
sun — molecules wedge freeze expand fall
heat on heat gristly gritty sledge-bearing
drop-wedging shards break fragmental fila-

ment shudders separates a hairbreadth crack
topples monoliths to waiting grating rock

QUICKSILVER (SEE MERCURY)

— R —

RAINBOW QUARTZ [SEE ROCK CRYSTAL]

RED TIGER'S EYE

❖ Naturally occurring TIGER'S EYE QYARTZ dyed to a deep brick or iron red

RHODOCHROSITE, MANGANESE SPAR, DIALOGITE

❖ While occasionally faceted, crystalline rhodochrosite is relatively soft and brittle, limiting its usefulness. Massive rhodochrosite is often carved or sliced to reveal pink-and-white concentric designs

❖ The concentric patterns derive from rhodochrosite stalactites, the best examples coming from Argentina

❖ Gem-quality rhodochrosite is a deep rose-red, frequently translucent

❖ Commercially, a source of manganese

❖ Occasionally crystals faceted as collectors' specimens, especially larger crystals (first discovered in 1974) from the Kalahari Desert in South Africa

❖ Crystals occasionally cut into cameos, polished as cabochons, or fashioned into beads

❖ Bull's-eye slabs of rhodochrosite layered with GALENA and PYRITES polished as collectors' specimens

❖ As of 2002, the state mineral of Colorado, since the finest large, red crystals are found in the Sweet Home Mine in that state

➤ *Dialogite*: Greek, *dialog* 'selection' + *ite* 'rock or mineral'

- ➢ *Inca Rose*: Refers to stones from Argentina, one of the oldest locations for rhodochrosite
- ➢ *Rhodochrosite*: German, *Rhodochrosit*, from Greek, *rhodo* 'rose' + *khroos* or *chros*, 'skin,' 'coloring'—'rose-colored' + *ite* 'mineral or rock'

- • Associated with Fire; Mercury-Uranus and Virgo; Jupiter and Sagittarius
- • Purifies blood
- • Enhances memory
- • Kept under the pillow, a Rhodochrosite crystal allows for more vivid and more easily remembered dreams
- • Traditionally considered a "stone of balance," balancing intellect/reason with intuition/emotion

RHODOLITE
- ❖ Red-pink variety of GARNET
- ❖ Mixture of pyrope and almandite, rose-red to purple, found in Macon County, North Carolina

- ➢ *Rhodolite*: Greek, *rhodo* 'rose' + *lite* 'mineral or rock'

RHODONITE, MANGANESE SPAR
- ❖ Visually differs from RHODOCHROSITE in being streaked with black (manganese); RHODOCHROSITE most often shows white (CALCITE) streaking
- ❖ Opaque to translucent, capable of a high polish
- ❖ Primarily cut *en cabochon* or fashioned into beads
- ❖ Transparent rhodonite rare, but occasionally faceted as collectors' specimens

- ➢ *Rhodonite*: Greek, *rhodon* 'rose' + *ite* 'mineral or rock'
- ➢ *Fowlerite*: Named for Dr. Samuel *Fowler* + *ite* 'rock or mineral'; brown- or –yellow-tinted variety containing zinc

- • Associated with Earth and Fire; Venus and Libra
- • Augments balance through strength of will

- Augments the consequences of cause and effect
- Encourages calmness and reflection
- Encourages generosity of spirit

RHYOLITE, RYOLITE

- ❖ Volcanic material analogous to granite, occasionally showing the banded flow lines of the original lava
- ❖ OBSIDIAN is a form of rhyolite that cooled so quickly that no crystals formed, resulting in natural glass

- ➢ *Rhyolite*: Greek, *rhyo-,* from Greek, *rhyax* 'stream of lava' + *ite* 'mineral or rock'
- ➢ *Orbicular Rhyolite*: Named for the circular eye-like patterns formed by internal crystals
- ➢ *Rainforest Rhyolite*: Named for the resemblance of its rich greens and yellows to an aerial view of a rain forest

- Pink-to-orange forms relate to female sexuality; brown-to-grey-to-purple, to male sexuality
- *Banded Rhyolite*: Anciently believed to heal circulatory and skin problems
- *Orbicular Rhyolite* Enhances the wearer's self-awareness, especially when gazing into the "eyes"

ROCK CRYSTAL

- ❖ Transparent, crystalline variety of QUARTZ
- ❖ Traditional gemstone for Monday

ROSE QUARTZ

- ❖ Light pink to deep pink variety of QUARTZ
- ❖ Earliest appearances: Assyria, circa 800 B.C.
- ❖ Rarely found in crystal form; almost all jewelry is cut from massive microcrystalline samples
- ❖ Rarely faceted, since the material is almost always cloudy, but common and popular cut *en cabochon* or as beads

- ➢ *Rose Quartz*: Named for its distinctive color

- Enhances love and heals emotional trauma; brings its wearer love
- Protects and heals relationships
- Enhances natural desires to remain faithful

FALLING WATER

Falling water cuts cold granite at its
Precipice—severe sharp glinting Mica,
Feldspar tumbled over milk-pink quartz,
Enough to make the summer sunlight ache—

Hovers…then down past draughty caverns
Vastly ancient, twisting about itself
In columns solid with an evanescent
Play of light and flash and flesh and lift—

Defies shoulders shudders sheers of face-cliffs
Barely visual—to plunge ecstatic
Cold and boiling into substance cleft
And cloven woven with all-shades of life—

Into the ceaseless blue of silent music…
Calmly warming blue-lit cool mosaic

RUBY
- ❖ Formed by chromium substitutions in colorless CORUNDUM
- ❖ Middle Ages: Colorless SAPPHIRES believed to be rubies that needed to be buried again in order to "ripen"; flawed rubies were considered over-ripe.
- ❖ Anciently, all clear red stones were classified as *carbunculus*; many historically famous "rubies"—including the "Black Prince's Ruby" in the British Crown Jewels—were identified in the 18th and 19th centuries as SPINEL and TOURMALINE instead.
- ❖ Because large flawless stones are extremely rare, a large ruby may exceed in value a DIAMOND, SAPPHIRE, or EMERALD of roughly the same size and clarity
- ❖ Only a few stones are large enough and important enough to

have received names; those that have include:

> Star of India: 536 carats, American Museum of Natural History, New York

> Star of Asia: 330 carats, Smithsonian Institution, Washington D.C.

❖ The largest gem-quality ruby, weighing 400 carats, was cut into three separate stones

❖ The record price for a single ruby was $5,860,000 for a 38.12 carat cabochon sold at public auction

❖ At 9.0 on the Mohs scale, RUBIES/CORUNDUM/SAPPHIRES are second only to DIAMOND in hardness

❖ Rubies included with RUTILE may show a three- or six-pointed star; such stones are cut as cabochons to emphasize the *asterism*

❖ Created or lab-grown rubies are fairly common and much less expensive than natural rubies; the primary difference between the two is that the synthetic varieties are uniformly flawless—all natural rubies contain some impurities or inclusions

❖ A synthetic ruby was used in the first laser

❖ Traditional birthstone for July and for the sign Leo

❖ Traditional gemstone for Tuesday

➢ *Ruby*: Latin, *rubinus*, 'red stone'; Latin, *ruber*, 'red'

• Anciently, associated with the Sun

• China: Assures the wearer's longevity

• Ancient Burma: Endows the owner with invulnerability when the ruby is inserted into the flesh

• Middle Ages: Contains an interior fire that could not be concealed

• 16th Century Europe: Protects the owner's health, removes evil thoughts, controls lust and excessive desire, evaporates vapors associated with pestilence and plague

• Believed to produce an internal heat sufficient to boil water

• Considered the Prince of Crystals, containing the heritage of humanity and the gift of humility

- Symbol of power and romance
- Symbol of passion and love
- Warns its owner of impending danger by becoming dark and dull, losing its brilliance
- Helps the physical body survive times of danger
- Associated with authority and leadership
- Encourages a sense of well-being and devotion to others
- Symbolizes eternal love and loyalty

RUTILE

- ❖ Although rutile forms crystals, it is relatively soft and thus is most valued as a gemstone when it appears as needle-like inclusions—gold, silver, black, or red—in other minerals, most notably QUARTZ and CORUNDUM (in which it causes *asterism* in star rubies and star sapphires)
- ❖ Classic rutile-in-quartz consists of parallel clusters of needles radiating star-like from a small polygonal plate of HEMATITE, all embedded in transparent QUARTZ
- ❖ Perfectly aligned golden rutile needles are sometimes called "Venus's Hair"
- ❖ Red to reddish-brown crystals, as large as several inches across, occasionally faceted, primarily as collectors' specimens
- ❖ Commercially, used in paints and fillers (especially as a white pigment), as a coating on welding rods, and as a primary source of titanium

- ➤ *Rutile*: German, *Rutil* 'red'; from Latin, *rutilus* 'reddish'
- ➤ *Titania*: Trade named for cut specimens of lab-grown rutile

- Associated with Fire and Earth; Mars-Pluto and Aries; Saturn and Capricorn
- Filters painful memories
- Adds power to whatever stone it includes
- Healing properties are enhanced when needle-like rutile crystals are embedded in QUARTZ (see RUTILATED QUARTZ)

Rutilated Quartz, Needle Stone
- Healing properties of QUARTZ enhanced by included rutile needles

Ryolite [See Rhyolite]

— S —

SAPPHIRE

❖ Blue sapphires are created by iron and titanium substitutions in colorless CORUNDUM

❖ Any transparent, gemmy variety of CORUNDUM except RUBY is considered a Sapphire, regardless of color

❖ Associated with DIAMOND, EMERALD, and RUBY as cardinal gemstones

❖ Sapphires colored other than blue are called *Fancy-color* sapphires

❖ Many lightly colored sapphires are heat-treated to intensify the natural color

❖ Star sapphires are included with needle-like crystals, often RUTILE, that will cause a six-pointed star to reflect in a cabochon-cut stone; this chatoyancy is called *asterism*

❖ Heating a star sapphire destroys *asterism* and creates a flawlessly clear, deeply colored stone

❖ Etruscans: first recorded use of sapphire, 7th Century B.C.

❖ Hebrews: One of the stones in the High Priest's Breastplate

❖ 11th Century: Favored stones for ecclesiastical rings

❖ 20th Century: Australia is the world's largest source of natural sapphires (about 75%)

❖ Specimens often cut in the country of origin

❖ Outstanding specimens include:

> *Star of India*: 563 carats; largest star sapphire known; presented to the American Museum of Natural History by J. P. Morgan in 1900; stolen by Jack Murphy, alias 'Murph the Surf', in 1964, but recovered shortly thereafter

> *Star of Asia*: 330 carats; second-largest star sapphire known;

Smithsonian Institution, Washington D.C.

Midnight Star: 117 carats; American Museum of Natural History

Stuart Sapphire: 104 carats (about 1 ½ inches long), set into the British Imperial State Crown

❖ Traditional birthstone for September and for the 45th wedding anniversary

❖ Traditional gemstone for Thursday

❖ Lab-grown sapphire, formed in large aluminum-oxide crystals called *boules*, is chemically identical to naturally formed crystals but generally flawless

➢ *Sapphire*: Latin, *sapphirus,* from the Greek, *sáppheiros,* possibily from Hebrew *sappir*, 'a precious stone', whose ultimate etymology and meaning is unknown

➢ *Sapphire*: Perhaps Sanskrit, *Sani* 'Saturn (Planet) + *priya* 'precious'—stone precious to Saturn

➢ Until the Middle Ages, *sapphirus,* meaning simply 'blue,' was the accepted name for Lapis Lazuli

➢ *African Sapphire*: Variety with lighter, more pastel blue shades

➢ *Burmese Sapphire*: Commonly refers to high quality, intense blue transparent stones with a suggestion of violet

➢ *Ceylon Sapphire*: Found on Sri Lanka; bright, light blue with subtle grey or violet shades

➢ *Kashmire Sapphire*: Commonly refers to light cornflower blue, medium transparent stones

➢ *Padparascha Sapphire*: Sinhalese, 'lotus flower'; name of a particularly fine orange-pink sapphire, often considered more valuable than blue sapphires

➢ *Thai Sapphire*: Commercial name for very dark blue specimens

• Anciently: Protects kings from jealousy, envy, and danger

• Persian mythology: The world stands on a single gigantic sapphire; its reflection accounts for the blue sky

• Hindus: Dwells in the roots of the World Tree

• India: A supernatural stone enhancing the relationship between gems and planets, with blue sapphire associated with Saturn, yellow sapphire associated with Jupiter

- Early Christians: Associated with the sky, hence a sacred stone
- 13th Century Europe: Has the power to vanquish poverty
- 15th Century Italy: A sapphire engraved with the appropriate planet image [Jupiter] and magical inscriptions would grant the wearer the virtues of the planet, that is, would make the wearer more "Jovial"
- 17th Century Germany: the *Siegstein,* or "Stone of Victory"
- Sri Lanka: Star sapphire a protection against witchcraft
- Jewel of Truth and Wisdom
- Associated with heavenly devotion and spiritual growth
- Traditionally considered a "stone of prosperity"
- Believed to be capable of controlling physical and emotional passions
- *Star Sapphire*: "Stone of Destiny"—its triple crossed lines represent Faith, Hope, and Destiny
- *Star Sapphire*: The star also symbolizes the Star of Bethlehem.
- *Star Sapphire*: Efficacious in transforming hopes and dreams into reality

SARD
- ❖ Transparent variety of CHALCEDONY, colored light brown by iron oxide and hydroxide inclusions
- ❖ Used by the Mycenaeans and Assyrians, circa 1400 B.C.
- ❖ Frequently used anciently for cylinder-seals, scarabs, and cut or carved gems, cameos, and intaglios
- ❖ Possibly one of the stones (*sardius)* in the High Priest's Breastplate

- ➤ *Sard*: Greek, *Sardeis,* capital of Lydia, Asia Minor—the Sardian stone
- ➤ *Sard*: Persian, *sered,* 'yellow'

- 11th Century Europe: Potent as a medicine

- Protected against sorcery and incantations
- New Age: Associated with home and family

SARDONYX [SEE SARD, ONYX]
❖ White and red or brown banded stone, the red bands being SARD, the lighter bands ONYX or some other stone
❖ Usually cut into cameos or cabochons to emphasize the parallel banding

➢ *Sardonyx*: *sard* + *onyx*

SCAPOLITE, WERNERITE
❖ Colorless, white, pink, violet, blue, and yellow transparent crystals and opaque massive materials
❖ Pink and violet specimens *pleochroic,* showing pink or violet from one direction, dark blue or lavender from another

➢ *Scapolite*: Latin, *scapus* 'stalk', from Greek, 'stick stone', reference to the crystal habit
➢ *Wernerite*: From A. G. *Werner*, a German mineralogist + *ite* 'rock or mineral'

SCHEELITE
❖ Important ore of tungsten
❖ Faceted crystals popular with collectors, occasionally used as gemstones
❖ Yellow, brown, orange, or colorless crystals
❖ For some time a popular DIAMOND simulant

➢ *Scheelite*: Named for K. W. *Scheel* + *ite* 'rock or mineral'

SCHORL [SEE TOURMALINE]

SERPENTINE
❖ Commonly green with an oily or silky luster, but may also be reddish, pink, black, grey, lavender, or almost white
❖ Frequently translucent
❖ Since it is relatively soft, frequently used in decorative carvings
❖ In various cultures, used for dagger hilts, knife handles, amulets,

caskets, bowls and vases, etc.

➢ *Serpentine*: Middle English, *serpentyn,* from Middle Latin, *serpentinus,* 'snake-like'; refers to the resemblance of its green-and-white surface to a serpent's skin

➢ *Antigorite*: From the Valle de *Antigorio* in Northern Italy, where it was first discovered + *ite* 'rock or mineral'; brownish-green variety of serpentine

➢ *Bowenite*: Named for G. T. *Bowen,* a geologist; translucent green variety of antigorite serpentine hard enough to be used for jewelry or ornamentation; used also as a JADE substitute

➢ *Tangiwai*: Maori, 'tears'; dark green bowenite formerly carved into ornaments by the Maori, rarely found today

➢ *Williamsite*: Soft variety of serpentine, oil-green with multiple black inclusions

• Associated with Earth and Water; Venus-Neptune and Pisces

• Protects against serpent bites and insect bites; can be used to draw toxins out of a snake bite—but only when the stone is in its natural state and has never touched contact iron

• *Chartreuse Serpentine*: pale yellow, reduces allergic reactions to animals, birds, and other pets

SEPTARIAN NODES, UTAH SEPTARIANS

❖ Concretions or nodules, often spherical or ovoid, containing angular cavities (*septaria*)

❖ Utah septarian nodules are frequently lined with brown CALCITE and filled with ARAGONITE crystals, separated from each other by dividing walls of bentonite clay

❖ Frequently used as paperweights, especially with the nodules fractured to show the different layering

❖ Used in eggs, spheres, fetish carving and cabochon jewelry

➢ *Septarium*: Latin, *septarium* 'enclosure'

• Concretions act as depositories of energy

• Contains other attributes related to CALCITE and ARAGONITE

SHELL

❖ A variety of aquatic animal shells used in jewelry, including in making buttons, beads, inlay, knife handles, and other ornaments:

> *Giant Conch*: Pink-and-white layers frequently cut into cameos

> *Helmet Shell*: Used in making cameos

> *Pearl Oysters*: Produce MOTHER-OF-PEARL, cut and carved into buttons, beads, and other ornaments

> *Paua Shell*: Produce vividly colored MOTHER-OF-PEARL

SILLIMANITE [SEE FIBROLITE]

❖ Pale blue or green, often fibrous (hence the name)

❖ *Pleochroic*; from different directions, crystals show as pale green, dark green, and blue

❖ Frequently tumbled as well as cut as cabochons or faceted

❖ Identical chemical composition to that of KYANITE and ANDALUSITE but with different crystalline structure

➢ *Sillimanite*: Named for Professor Benjamin *Silliman* of Yale University + *ite* 'rock or mineral'

➢ *Bucholzite*: Alternate name for sillimanite

➢ *Fibrolite*: From *fibro*, from its fibrous texture + *lite* 'rock or mineral'

SILVER

❖ An element as well as a precious metal

❖ One of the earliest metals used by humans, since it is a free element (that is, occurs in a nearly pure state) and is relatively easy to separate from its ores

❖ Probably discovered after GOLD and COPPER

❖ Some silver artifacts found in Egypt are nearly 5,500 years old

❖ Written records in India refer to silver nearly 3,000 years ago

❖ India: Some foods still decorated with a thin layer of silver, called *Varak*

❖ Symbolizes the Moon

❖ Symbolizes Venus in the Renaissance magical Triad of Sol and

- ❖ Long a staple in minting coins but now too valuable for that use
- ❖ In spite of its traditional value as second only to GOLD, silver has no common rhyme-word in English
- ❖ Second only to DIAMOND among natural minerals as a conductor of heat and electricity, first among all metals
- ❖ Combined with 7.5% brass to create *sterling silver*, with GOLD a staple in jewelry making

- ➤ *Silver*: Old English, *seolfor,* possibly from Germanic **silubhra*; from Akkadian, *sarapu,* 'refine, smelt'
- ➤ *Argentium*: Scientific name for silver, from Latin, *argos,* 'shiny' or 'white'

- • One of the seven metals associated with Alchemy
- • Associated with Venus
- • Hippocrates: Efficacious in healing and preventing disease
- • Associated with purity and therefore helps cure numerous maladies
- • Traditionally repels vampires, because of its association with holy objects; vampires cannot see their reflections in mirrors because of the silver backing
- • Traditionally, silver bullets kill werewolves
- • Silver lockets ward off danger
- • Facilitates physical, emotional, and mental cleansing
- • Displays gentle, calming effects
- • Protects the wearer, particularly during travel

SINHALITE
- ❖ Pale yellow-brown to dark green-brown crystals
- ❖ Originally considered a brown variant of PERIDOT: identified as separate stone in 1952
- ❖ Pleochroic, showing pale brown, green-brown, and dark brown when viewed from different directions
- ❖ Most specimens found as tumbled pebbles in gem gravels
- ❖ Gem-quality sinhalite usually faceted

> *Sinhalite*: Sanscrit, *'sinhala'* ancient name for Sri Lanka + *ite* 'rock or mineral'

SMOKY QUARTZ, CAIRNGORM, MORION, COON TAIL QUARTZ

❖ Earliest sources: Sumeria, as an ornamental stone, circa 3,100 B.C.

❖ Formed naturally or artificially by irradiating QUARTZ containing aluminum

❖ With smoky TOPAZ, one of the few brown or black minerals used as gemstones; others—including black BERYL and brown CORUNDUM—are extremely rare

❖ May be yellow to dark brown or black

❖ A particularly dark, opaque form is known as *Morion*

> *Cairngorm Stone*: so named for *Cairngorm* Mountains in Scotland

> *Coon Tail Quartz*: Smoky quartz showing alternating black and grey banding

> *Morion*: Latin, *morion,* a misreading of *mormorion,* a kind of crystal

• Anciently: Aids in divination and *scrying* (forecasting the future using a crystal ball)

• Stone of protection, both at home and away

• Wards off depression, anger, negative energy

• Serves as a grounding stone

SOAPSTONE [SEE TALC]

SODALITE

❖ One of the major components of LAPIS LAZULi (contributing a rich, royal blue color)

❖ May also be grey, green, pink, or mottled

❖ Uses in jewelry include ornamental carvings and cutting into cabochons, beads, and ornamental items

Sodalite: Medieval Latin, *soda* 'barilla' (from which soda is made) + *ite* 'rock or mineral'; so named for its sodium content

Bluestone, Canadian bluestone: Alternative name

Hackmanite: Pale to deep pink variety; exhibits *tenebrescence*, that is, the color changes on exposure to sunlight, from pink to grey-white or white to pink, depending on the source location

Molybdosodalite: Variety containing less chlorine and a slight percentage of molybdenum oxide

Princess Blue: Early name for sodalite, so called because it was first discovered in Canada during a Royal visit

- Associated with Air and Water; Moon and Cancer; Mercury and Gemini; Saturn-Uranus and Aquarius
- Balances metabolism
- Acts as a record-keeper, preserving new ideas and emotions
- Facilitates logic and truth
- Cooling when used with burns and inflammations

SPECTROLITE [SEE LABRADORITE]

SPHALERITE, BLENDE, ZINC BLENDE, BLACK-JACK, MARMATITE

❖ Primary source of zinc
❖ Known since ancient times
❖ Only occasionally cut as a gemstone; because the mineral is soft, it is primarily used for collectors' specimens
❖ Dispersion—'fire'—exceeds that of DIAMOND
❖ Colorless unless it contains IRON
❖ May also be red, yellow, orange, brown, or green

➢ *Sphalerite*: German, *Sphalerit*, from Greek, *sphaleros* 'slippery, deceitful' from *sphallein* 'to trip' + *ite* 'rock or part of a rock'; so named because it may easily be mistaken for GALENA
➢ *Marmatite*: Particularly iron-rich variety

- Protects the wearer against treachery by enhancing the wearer's intuition

SPHENE, TITANITE

- ❖ Titanite the approved name for the mineral; gem specimens usually referred to as sphene
- ❖ Source of titanium oxide, used as a yellow pigment in artist's paints
- ❖ Gemstone specimens usually chartreuse
- ❖ Displays stronger 'fire' than DIAMOND
- ❖ Although brilliant, both brittle and soft (5.5 on the Mohs scale), limiting its use as a gemstone to pendants and brooches or as collectors' specimens
- ❖ Occasionally *pleochroic,* three colors appearing when the crystal is view from different directions

- ➢ *Sphene*: Greek, *sphen,* 'wedge'; so named for the characteristic shape of its crystals
- ➢ *Titanite*: From *titanium + ite* 'rock or mineral'

- Incorporates the four elements: Earth, Air, Fire, and Water
- Facilitates joining spirit with earth
- Enhances spirituality and compassion

SPINEL

- ❖ Earliest example: Ornament in a Buddhist temple in Afghanistan and in Rome, circa 1st Century B.C.
- ❖ Blue spinels recorded in England by 400 A. D.
- ❖ For centuries, true spinels were assumed to be either emeralds or rubies—spinel and corundum are found in the same deposits and have similar properties
- ❖ Red spinel is most valued as a gemstone and was frequently confused with RUBY; identified as a separate stone in 1779
- ❖ The *Black Prince's Ruby* in the British Imperial State Crown, is in fact one of the largest gem-quality spinels, nearly two inches in length, with a smaller inset RUBY
- ❖ The *Timur Ruby*, also set in the Imperial State Crown, 361 unfaceted stone, inscribed with the names of owners dating back to

1612, but known as early as 1398

❖ Blue and green transparent spinels also valued as gemstones

❖ Frequently included with RUTILE crystals, resulting in *asterism*, four- or six-rayed stars appearing when the stone is cut *en cabochon*

❖ The two largest rough spinels weigh 520 carats each

❖ Lab-grown spinels now common

➢ *Spina*: Italian, *spinella*, diminutive of Latin, *spina* 'spiny, thorny' a reference to internal 'spines' that infrequently cause asterism and to its sharp, pointed crystals

➢ *Balas, Balas Ruby*: From Persian, *Badakhshan*, a region near Samarkand where it was found; pale to rose-red variety

➢ *Chromite*: Black to brown iron-chromium variety

➢ *Franklinite*: Named for *Franklin*, New Jersey; black, magnetic variety composed of zinc, iron, zinc manganese

➢ *Gahnite, Gahnospinel, Zinc Spinel*: Named for Johan Gottlieb *Gahn*, a Swedish chemist (who discovered manganese) + ite 'rock or mineral'; rare blue, violet, dark green or black variety

➢ *Hercynite*: From Latin, *Hercynia silva* 'Hercynian forest north of the Danube + *ite* 'rock or mineral'; dark-green to black variety

➢ *Magnesiochromite*: Variety containing magnesium and chromium

➢ *Picotite, Chroie Spinel*: Brown, green, or black variety

➢ *Pleonaste, Ceylanite, Ceylonite*: From Greek, 'abundant, rich'; dark-green to black, opaque, iron-bearing variety

➢ *Rubicel, Rubicellel*: French, *rubacelle*, from Latin *rubeus, 'red, reddish';* earlier name for yellow, orange, brown variety from Brazil

• Romans: Considered as rubies, with the same powers

• Middle Ages: *Red spinel* efficacious against bleeding, hemorrhages, and inflammatory diseases (because of the belief in *sympathetic magic* and the relation between the red of the spinel and the red of blood)

- 17th Century India: A potion of powdered spinel eliminates foreboding and assures happiness
- Soothes anger, conflict, and other 'heated' emotions (again associating the color of the gem with the 'color' of the emotion)
- Calms and alleviates stress, particularly blue and green spinels
- *Red spinel* enhances strength

SPODUMENE
- ❖ Discovered in 1877 in Brazil
- ❖ Source of lithium used in ceramics, mobile phones, and automotive batteries
- ❖ Transparent varieties have long been valued as gemstones, although difficult to cut effectively
- ❖ Rarely displays cat's eye effect

- ➢ *Spodumene*: German, *Spodumen,* from Greek, *spodumenos* 'burnt to ashes', from *spodos* 'wood ash'; for the opaque, ashy appearance of non-gemstone materials
- ➢ *Hiddenite*: Pale to deep green variety; *pleochroic,* showing blue-green, emerald green, and yellow-green when viewed from different directions
- ➢ *Kunzite*: Pink to lilac variety; *pleochroic*, showing colorless and shades of violet when viewed from different directions

STAUROLITE, CROSS STONE
- ❖ Identified as a separate species in 1792
- ❖ One of the few gemstones naturally forming right-angle crosses, another being ANDALUSITE
- ❖ Naturally occurs in 90° and 60° crosses, suggesting the Maltese, Roman, and St. Andrews Crosses
- ❖ Frequently occurs in MICA schists, often studded with small natural GARNETS
- ❖ Occurs in only a few areas of the world: Georgia, North Carolina, Switzerland, New Mexico, and New Hampshire
- ❖ Official state mineral of Georgia
- ❖ So popular that unscrupulous dealers carve forgeries from simi-

lar materials

- > *Staurolite:* Greek, *stauros* 'cross' + *-lithos* 'stone

- Associated with Christianity and may be seen to have the same effects as other crosses
- Commonly known as "Fairy Crosses" or "Fairy Stones"
- Georgia: The natural crosses mark the tears shed by the Cherokee as they were driven from their homeland on the "Trail of Tears"
- Crystals protect against negativity
- Crystals energize sexual drives
- Considered good luck stones; staurolite crosses carried by Presidents Roosevelt, Wilson, and Harding

STEATITE [SEE TALC]

STICHTITE

- ❖ Pink, lilac, and purple massive material, primarily decomposed chromium-rich SERPENTINE
- ❖ Occasionally cut *en cabochon*, particularly vibrantly colored specimens

- > *Stichtite*: Named after Robert Carl *Sticht*, manager of a mine near the discovery site in Tasmania in 1910 + *ite* 'rock or mineral'

STILBITE

- ❖ One of the ZEOLITES
- ❖ More of a collector's specimen than a gemstone

- > *Stilbite*: Greek, *stilb-,* root of *stilbein*, 'to shine'

- New Age: Associated with Aries
- Encourages love, energy, creativity, guidance and grounding
- Pink stilbite enhances loving, creative energies

STROMATOLITE

- ❖ Essentially FOSSILIZED marine algae, often displaying intricate patterns of light and dark banding that respond well to cutting and polishing
- ❖ Among the oldest known fossils, some well over 3,000,000,000 years old
- ❖ Stromatolites continue to form, particularly in western Australia

➢ *Stromatolite*: German, *Stromatolith,* from Late Latin, *stroma-, stromat-* 'covering' + *lite* 'rock or mineral'

SUGILITE, ALSO LUVULITE

- ❖ Only rarely faceted as a gemstone; more frequently used in its massive form for carvings and cabochons
- ❖ One of the deepest, most vivid naturally occurring purple minerals
- ❖ With CHAROITE and BERTRANDITE/Tiffany Stone, among the most valued purple minerals

➢ *Sugilite*: Named for Ken-ichi Sugi, the Japanese geologist who first identified sugilite in 1944, + *lite* 'rock or mineral'

- • Associated with Water and Earth; Mercury and Virgo; Jupiter and Sagittarius
- • Powerful healing stone, with qualities only recently discovered
- • "As sugilite evolves, it will prove to be a most effective medicine in the alternative treatments of cancer as well as AIDS and other sexually transmitted diseases (STDS)" (Elsbeth 196)

SULFUR

- ❖ The spelling 'sulphur' no longer accepted in scientific journals
- ❖ Analogous to the Biblical "Brimstone"
- ❖ Contemporary uses include as a component of gunpowder, matches, and fireworks; in fertilizers; and as a treatment for certain skin conditions
- ❖ One of its products, sulfuric acid, is among the most common chemicals in the world

- ❖ Early nineteenth-century matches, based on sulfur, were called *lucifers*, presumably because of their strong smell; subsequently phosphorus was added, eliminating much of the odor
- ❖ Sulfur provides the rich gold coloring in iron sulfide, commonly known as PYRITE or fool's gold

- ➢ *Sulfur*: Latin, *sulphur*

- • Associated with Fire; Pluto and Scorpio
- • Known and used since prehistoric times
- • Ancient Egypt: Used in hot springs as a health treatment
- • Considered healing for all wounds
- • 15th Century Italy, philosopher Marsilio Ficino taught that all metals were generated by the vapor of sulfur mixed with the vapor of *argent vive* (that is, *Quick-silver* or MERCURY)
- • Other Renaissance philosophers contended that there were only two elements—sulfur and MERCURY
- • New Age: Rejuvenates the user

SUNSTONE, AVENTURINE FELDSPAR
- ❖ Oligoclase FELDSPAR with vivid metallic red-gold inner sheen when viewed from certain directions
- ❖ The flash of color comes from reflections from inclusions of HEMATITE or GOETHITE plates parallel to the cleavage plane
- ❖ Cut *en cabochon*
- ❖ Some have proposed that the Vikings used sunstone to determine the direction of the sun's rays for navigating

- ➢ *Sunstone*: Named for its suggestion of the sun's brilliance

- • Rejuvenates the spirit

— T —

TAAFFEITE, TAAFEITE, MAGNESIOTAAFFEITE
- ❖ One of the rarest of gemstones, with uncut specimens even rarer than cut ones
- ❖ Unique as the only gemstone first identified from a cut and faceted specimen
- ❖ Between 1945 and 1967, only four specimens found
- ❖ To date only a few additional stones have been found, apparently all originally from Sri Lanka or Tanzania
- ❖ One recent internet site offered a 1.66 carat white taaffeite for over $1,000; another offered a light violet 5.01 carat pear cut stone for $18,036.00

- ➢ *Taaffeite*: Named for Count R. *Taaffe* of Dublin, who discovered the first cut stone in a box of miscellaneous stones in 1945 + *ite* 'rock or mineral'

TALC, TALCUM, STEATITE, SOAPSTONE
- ❖ Fine-grained, green-to-grey, soft mineral
- ❖ The softest mineral on the Mohs scale of hardness, capable of being scratched by a fingernail
- ❖ Used for millennia as a carving or sculpting material
- ❖ As steatite or soapstone (massive, granular talc), used for carving of furniture, ornaments and jewelry
- ❖ Steatite can often be carved with a sharp knife

- ➢ *Soapstone*: So named for its soapy or greasy feel
- ➢ *Steatite*: Latin *steatites*, from the Greek root *steat*-, 'fat or tallow' + *ite* 'rock or mineral', so named for its greasy feel
- ➢ *Talc*: from Arabic *talq* and Persian *talk,* 'talc' or 'mica'

TANZANITE

❖ Blue-violet-purple variety of ZOISITE, the color caused by traces of vanadium in the stone

❖ Pleochroic; crystals change color when viewed from different directions or under different light sources (natural vs. incandescent, for example)

❖ Most tanzanite is heat-treated to enhance the natural color

❖ Available as a gemstone since its discovery in 1967

❖ In 2002, added to the birthstone charts as birthstone for December

❖ In 2003, Tanzania passed legislation banning the export of uncut Tanzanite to Jaipur, India, where most tanzanite gemstones had previously been cut

❖ Since 2005, prices for tanzanite have increased following one company's increasing assumption of control over mined rough

❖ Prices have raised from $425 per carat in 2000 to nearing $2000 in 2007

❖ Since tanzanite occurs primarily in a single location, there is a chance that the deposit might become exhausted, ending its availability

❖ Several simulants are available, including lab-grown crystals and colored CUBIC ZIRCONIA

➤ *Tanzanite*: Named for *Tanzania,* the site of its discovery + *ite* 'rock or mineral'; named by a vice-president of Tiffany & Company

• Considered a calming stone

• Provides balance for highly focused and driven people or obsessively creative people

• When set in GOLD, it balances the moon's energies and the sun's

TEKTITE [SEE ALSO MOLDAVITE]

❖ Generally accepted to be of extraterrestrial origin—tektites occur in groups in widely scattered locations, with no relation to local geological strata

❖ Alternatively, though to be of volcanic origin, although many specimens come from locales show no other evidence of volcanic activity

❖ Earlier: Suggested that tektites were "fired" toward the Earth by volcanic explosions on the moon—not a widely supported suggestion

❖ Roughly 750,000 gathered worldwide

❖ Usually dark-brown or dark-green transparent nodules, about walnut-sized, with a rough or knobbly texture, composed of silicon glass

❖ Frequently pitted, which gives tektites an intriguing surface for wire-wrapping as jewelry

❖ Occasionally faceted, resembling bottle-green PERIDOT

❖ Varieties occasionally named after the locations where they were discovered

➢ *Tektite*: German, *tektite*, from Greek, *tektos*, 'molten' + *ite* 'rock or mineral'

➢ *Australite*: Named for *Australia*; found in southern Australia and Tasmania

➢ *Bediasite*: Named for *Bedias*, a town in Eastern Texas; black variety associated with the 34,000,000 year-old Chesapeake Bay impact crater

➢ *Billitonite:* Named for *Billiton/Belitung*, Indonesia, near Borneo

➢ *Georgiaite*: Named for the state of *Georgia*, USA; green variety also associated with the Chesapeake Bay impact crater

➢ *Indochinite*: Variety found in Cambodia, Laos, Thailand, and Vietnam

➢ *Javaite*: Variety found in Java

➢ *Malaysianite*: Variety found in Malaysia

➢ *Moldavite*: Named for the *Moldau* River in Bohemia (Czechoslovakia) near where they were first discovered in 1787

➢ *Philippinite*: Variety found in the Philippines and southern China; most common form of tektite, accounting for roughly 2/3 of the specimens

• Encourages rationality and sensibility

THULITE, ALSO ROSALINE

❖ A rich pink, manganese-rich variety of ZOISITE
❖ Used in carving jewelry and other ornaments

➢ *Thulite*: Named after *Thule,* a legendary island in the far north + *ite* 'rock or mineral'; first discovered in Norway, thought by some to be the original *Thule*

• Enhances dexterity; valuable to craftsmen

TIGER'S EYE QUARTZ [SEE HAWK'S EYE, IRON EYE, PIETERSITE]

❖ Valued for its *chatoyancy*, its cat's-eye effect
❖ Usually fibrous yellow/gold and brown
❖ The gold fibers are formed by silicified (altered or chemically converted into silica) CROCIDOLITE (blue asbestos); insufficiently altered CROCIDOLITE results in blue HAWK'S EYE
❖ Occasional pieces show CROCIDOLITE in transitional stages, with both blue and gold fibrous patterns in a single stone
❖ Fiber-optic glass—called cat's eye glass—imitates natural tiger's eye
❖ Usually cut *en cabochon* to highlight the chatoyancy

➢ *Tiger's Eye*: Named for its resemblance to vertical pupils in tigers' eyes.

• Associated with both Earth (brown) and Sun (gold)
• Accentuates self-confidence and self-assurance
• Promotes self-awareness
• Enhances wealth and protects from illness and other dangers
• Aids in creativity and decision-making
• New Age: Particularly effective when set in COPPER

TIGER IRON

❖ Combination of red JASPER and black HEMATITE in undulating contrasting bands; may contain fibrous CROCODILITE as well

- ❖ Such deposits are more than 2,000,000,000 years old
- ❖ Used for jewelry and ornaments
- ❖ Because it is heavy, dark colored, and strongly banded, often used in men's jewelry

TIN [SEE CASSITERITE]

- ❖ One of the seven metals associated with Alchemy
- ❖ Symbolizes the planet Jupiter
- ❖ Cassiterite is a primary ore of tin

- ➤ *Cassiterite*: Greek, *kasiteros,* 'tin' + *ite* 'rock or mineral'
- ➤ *Tin*: Old Norse, *tin*, German, *Zinn*

- • One of the seven metals associated with Alchemy
- • Symbolizes the planet Jupiter

TITANITE [SEE SPHENE]

TOPAZ

- ❖ The world's largest crystal, discovered in Brazil in 1940, weighs just under 600 pounds
- ❖ The largest cut topaz weighs 36,853 carats
- ❖ May be colorless or shades of yellow, blue, or green
- ❖ In the Middle Ages, the name applied to any yellow stone
- ❖ Yellow topaz the traditional November birthstone
- ❖ Some varieties, especially yellow-brown, fade gradually in sunlight
- ❖ Pink variety most frequently heat-treated yellow crystals
- ❖ Transparent *Braganza Topaz* in the Portuguese Royal Crown (1,600 carats, 11 oz.) originally thought to be a DIAMOND
- ❖ Largest cut yellow topaz, the *American Topaz*, with 172 facets, weighs 22, 892.5 carats (4.58 kg; 10.10 lbs.); Smithsonian Institution, Washington D.C.; cutting took over two years to complete
- ❖ Crystal weighing 3,270 carats (23 oz.) owned by the Smithsonian Institution in Washington, D.C.
- ❖ Traditional gemstone for Sagittarius

- ❖ Traditional gemstone for Scorpio
- ❖ Traditional gemstone for Sunday

- ➢ *Topaz*: Sanskrit, *tapaz*, 'fire'
- ➢ *Topaz*: Greek, *Topazios,* an island in the Red Sea (now called Zebirget) where a yellow gemstone (probably not topaz) was found anciently

- Associated with Air and Fire; Venus and Taurus; Mercury and Gemini; Jupiter and Sagittarius
- Greeks: Wearing the stone enhanced strength
- Believed to ward off sudden death
- Middle Ages: Strengthens the mind; prevents sudden death
- Middle Ages: Recommended by Hildegard von Bingen as a cure for loss of vision
- Believed to make the wearer invisible when necessary
- 11th Century: Topaz immersed in wine for three days, then laid on an inflamed eye, cures vision problems
- 13th Century: Ensures the good will of kings and princes, particularly when engraved with the image of a falcon
- 15th Century: Used as a cure for plague
- Acts as a cure for madness
- Aids in relieving stress
- Placing a crystal beneath the bed at night facilitates revitalization
- Stimulates positive dreams
- Beneficial for the lungs

TOPAZOLITE
GARNET variety resembling TOPAZ in color

TOURMALINATED QUARTZ, TOURMALINE IN QUARTZ

❖ Clear QUARTZ with included black, occasionally deep green, needles of TOURMALINE
❖ While not as spectacular as RUTILATED QUARTZ, nonetheless impressive for its stark contrasts

• Brings the forces of light and dark into balance
• Inclusions are augmented in power by the clear QUARTZ matrix

TOURMALINE

❖ Earliest sources: India, 1st or 2nd Centuries B.C.
❖ When heated, tourmaline crystals develop an electrical charge, positive at one end of the crystal, negative at the other; hence tourmaline tends to draw dust and becomes difficult to keep clean in museums, etc.
❖ Originally called *aschentrekker* ('ash puller) by the Dutch because of the electrical effect; they used heated tourmaline to clean ash from meerschaum pipes
❖ High quality stones among the rarest precious gems
❖ Single-colored crystals quite rare; most show several colors within a single crystal
❖ *Schorl* is the most common variety, accounting for 95% or so of all naturally occurring tourmaline

➢ *Schorl*: Named for a village in Saxony, Germany, now known as Zschorlau
➢ *Tourmaline*: Greek, *turmalin,* from Sinhalese, *turmali, toramalli* 'something little out of the earth'; Sinhalese, *toramalliya,* carnelian
➢ *Achroic* or *Achroite*: Colorless tourmaline; quite rare but the least expensive form of the gemstone
➢ *Buergerite*: Named after Martin J. Buerger, American professor at MIT; iron-bearing variety
➢ *Canary Tourmaline*: Yellow tourmaline
➢ *Cat's eye Tourmaline:* Pink and green varieties show the strong-

est *chatoyancy*

➤ *Chrome Tourmaline*: Rare form of green dravite tourmaline, colored by chromium (which also gives EMERALD its deep green)

➤ *Dichroic Tourmaline*: Crystals change color when viewed from different directions

➤ *Dravite*: Dark yellow to brownish black; from the Drave area of Carinthia (southern Austria)

➤ *Elbaite*: Lithium-based form that includes rubellite, indicolite, verdelite, and achroite

➤ *Indicolite,* or *Brazilian Sapphire*: From *indigo*: blue tourmaline, occasionally deep enough in color to mask the stone's gem-like qualities

➤ *Liddicoatite*: Calcium-bearing variety

➤ *Paraiba* or *Neon*: Vivid blue and green tourmaline recently discovered in Brazil

➤ *Rubellite*: Red and pink tourmaline

➤ *Schorl*: Black, usually opaque, tourmaline

➤ *Siberite*: Named after *Siberia* + *ite* 'rock or mineral'; lilac to violet-blue variety

➤ *Tsilaisite*: Named for a locality in Madagascar; magnesium variety

➤ *Uvite*: Green, brown, red or pink tourmaline

➤ *Verdelite* or *Brazilian Emerald*: Green tourmaline

➤ *Watermelon Tourmaline*: bicolor crystals with a green rind and pink core, found in Brazil; similar stones from California have a pink rind and green core

• Associated with Air, Earth, and Fire; Mercury and Virgo; Jupiter and Sagittarius

• As a relatively recent (late 19th Century) gemstone, tourmaline has few legends associated with it; its earliest chief proponent, George F. Kunz, argued against its proposed use as an alternative birthstone for October

• Colored tourmalines take on the powers associated with the colors themselves; for example, *green tourmaline* encourages physical regeneration and rebirth

- *Black Tourmaline/Schorl*: protects its wearer from black magic by turning away magic and negative energies

TSAVORITE

❖ Rarest variety of grossular GARNET, colored by vanadium or chromium; among the most expensive varieties of GARNET

❖ Restricted initially to Tanzania, then subsequently found in Kenya and later in Madagasgar

❖ Introduced as a precious gemstone in 1974 by Tiffany & Company

❖ The largest yet discovered weighs over 325 carats

➢ *Tsavorite*: Named for the *Tsavo National Park* in Kenya + *ite* 'rock or mineral'

TURQUOISE

❖ Fashioned into beads in Mesopotamia (ancient Iran and Iraq), circa 5,000 B.C.

❖ Among the first gemstones mined: Sinai Peninsula, circa 3,000 B.C.; among the first imitated, circa 3100 B.C.

❖ Susceptible to weathering, dirt, grease, heat. and sunlight, which alters blue turquoise to a muddy green; hence most gemstone turquoise is *stabilized*, that is, treated with wax or oil to seal the naturally porous, chalky stone; more modern techniques for impregnation with epoxy or plastic may lessen the stone's value

❖ May be speckled with PYRITE or laced with limonite veins

❖ Did not become popular as a gemstone in the West until after the 1300s

❖ Most frequently cut as cabochons for use in pendants, necklaces, earrings, rings, and bracelets

❖ Frequently imitated by natural stones (such as dyed HOWLITE or MAGNESITE) and artificial glasses or plastics

❖ Traditional gemstone for Sagittarius

❖ Traditional gemstone for Saturday

❖ Iran's national gemstone

➢ *Turquoise*: 13th Century France, *pierre turquoise* 'Turkish stone' or *Pierre turquin* 'dark-blue stone'

➤ *Odontolite*: Fossilized tooth or bone naturally colored by VIVI-ANITE, formerly mined in France as a turquoise substitute

- Associated with Earth and Air; Venus, Neptune and Libra
- Persia: The new moon reflected from turquoise brings luck
- Persia: Essentially the national stone for several thousand years, often used to decorate buildings
- Persia: Turquoise stones engraved with sacred words
- Hindus: To look at the new moon, then immediately thereafter to look at turquoise, insures great wealth
- Turquoise changes colors to reflect the wearer's health
- Middle Ages: Archetypal 'horse-amulet' to protect horses
- 13th Century: Turquoise protects the wearer from being thrown from a horse, falling from a house, or having a wall fall on the wearer's head—properties enhanced if the turquoise is set in GOLD
- 17th Century Europe: Essentially a masculine stone; women rarely wore it
- 17th Century England: Believed to signal the wearer's health by its color change; the poet John Donne wrote:

  > As a compassionate turquoise which doth tell
  > By looking pale the wearer is not well.[2]

- American Indians: Considered a sacred stone because of its power to protect and to heal; essential to a healer's or shaman's equipment
- American Indians: Reminder of the importance of the human spirit
- Pueblo, Apache, Navajo: important as an amulet stone
- Pueblo tribe: Restricted to men until the beginning of the 18th Century
- Navajos: Thrown into a river, accompanied by appropriate

---

[2] Donne, *The First Anniversary,* lines 343-344.

prayers, insured rain

- Apaches: Attached to an arrow assured accurate aim
- Associated with courage and strength
- Changes color to reveal a wife's infidelity
- Attached to a string and vibrated against glass, tells time accurately
- Excellent for conducting healing energies, due largely to its COPPER content

— U —

ULEXITE

❖ Extremely soft material, ranging from 1 to 2 ½ on the Mohs scale depending upon the composition of each specimen

❖ Called the 'television stone' since a piece of fibrous ulexite, viewed along the cross-sections of its long crystals, will slightly magnify and transmit images on the surface beneath it

➤ *Ulexite*: Named for Georg Ludwig *Ulex*, a 19th-Century German chemist who fiorst described it in 1850 + *ite* 'rock or mineral'

• Aids spiritual vision
• Encourages positivity

UNAKITE, EPIDOTIZED GRANITE, EPIDOSITE

❖ Striking stone, composed of green EPIDOTE, pink FELDSPAR, and clear QUARTZ

❖ One of the few semi-precious gemstones with a humorous nick-name, *Unakite* is also called—for obvious reasons of color and pattern—'spinach on a brick'

➤ *Unakite*: Named for the *Unakas Mountains* in North Carolina, site of the first discovery + *ite* 'rock or mineral'
➤ *Epidosite*: Similar material lacking QUARTZ

• Enables the wearer to direct the course of his/her own life
• Enables the wearer to enhance positive thoughts and eliminate negative feelings
• Associated with healthy pregnancies and reproductive functions

URALITE [SEE ACTINOLITE]

➢ *Uralite*: Named for the *Ural Mountains,* where it was discovered + *ite* 'rock or mineral'

UTAHLITE [SEE VARISCITE]

UVAROVITE

❖ Among the rarer members of the GARNET group
❖ Primarily notable as a consistently emerald-green crystal, although generally crystals are too small for use in jewelry
❖ Important as a collector's specimen

➢ *Uvarovite:* Named by its discoverer, Germain Henri Hess, after the Russian statesman Sergei Semenovitch *Uvarov* + *ite* 'rock or mineral'

• Stimulates the wearer's imagination

UVITE

❖ Colorless, green, or reddish- to yellowish-brown member of the TOURMALINE group
❖ Used primarily as collectors' specimens

➢ Named for the *Uva Province,* Sri Lanka, where it was first discovered + *ite* 'rock or mineral'

— V —

VANADINITE

- ❖ Bright red or orange crystals, primarily used as collectors' specimens
- ❖ Minor source of vanadium

- ➤ *Vanadinite*: *Vanad(ium)* + *in* + *ite* 'rock or mineral'
- ➤ *Vanadium*: Named for *Vanadis*, one of the names of Freya, Norse goddess of fertility, as well as beauty, war, death, prophecy, and wealth

- • Crystals promote spiritual inspiration

VARISCITE, UTAHLITE

- ❖ Identified as a distinct mineral in 1837
- ❖ Chemically similar to TURQUOISE, variscite ranges from pale green to emerald green, frequently interspersed with white streaks
- ❖ In the United States, located only in the western states, primarily Utah and Nevada
- ❖ One recent discovery, with coloration midway between TURQUOISE and variscite, has been dubbed 'variquoise' (demonstrating that occasionally geologists do have senses of humor)
- ❖ Quite soft (3 ½ to 4 ½ on the Mohs scale) and liable to lose its distinctive green color when polished
- ❖ Used primarily cut as cabochons or fashioned into beads

- ➤ *Variscite*: German, from *Variscia*, an ancient district in which the gemstone was first located, + *ite* 'mineral or rock'
- ➤ *Australian Turquoise*: Misnomer for Variscite crystals found in Queensland, Australia

- Encourages positive solutions to problems
- Amplifies self-confidence

VESUVIANITE, IDOCRASE

- ❖ Identified as a separate mineral in 1795
- ❖ Most commonly pale green, but also brown, yellow, blue, emerald green, white, red, purple, violet
- ❖ Sometimes faceted but primarily as collectors' specimens
- ❖ Brittle mineral, generally not suitable for jewelry

- ➢ *Vesuvianite*: Named for Mount *Vesuvius*, site of its initial discovery + *ite* 'rock or mineral'
- ➢ *Californite*, or *California Jade, American Jade, Vesuvianite-Jade*: Particularly jade-like green vesuvianite
- ➢ *Cyprine*: Blue variety colored by COPPER impurities, found near Franklin, New Jersey
- ➢ *Idocrase*: Older name for gem-quality vesuvianite
- ➢ *Wiluite*: Green variety found near Wilui, Siberia
- ➢ *Xanthite*: Yellow, manganese-rich form

- Balances and encourages competitiveness

VIVIANITE

- ❖ Used as a dye and as a collectors' specimen
- ❖ Exposure to light darkens the crystals' blue color
- ❖ Frequently found near PYRITE and COPPER
- ❖ Used as a pigment, blue ocher, by German painters in the 13th and 14th centuries
- ❖ Crystals are colorless until exposed to oxygen, which turns them blue

- ➢ *Vivianite*: named for J. G. *Vivian*, an English mineralogist who discovered it + *ite* 'rock or mineral'
- ➢ *Blue Iron Earth*: Former name, referring to its use in making a blue artist's pigment

- Crystals enhance the wearer's beauty

VOGESITE, VOEGESITE

❖ A combination of hornblende and FELDSPAR
❖ Associated with Capricorn
❖ Associated with the 2nd chakra, the "gateway of the moon."

• Enhances sexuality and procreation
• Tumbled stones protect from earthquakes
• Encourages unity in diversity

VOLCANIC ROCKS [LAVA]

❖ Associated with the Hawaiian volcano-goddess Pele

➤ *Volcano*: Latin, *Vulcan*, God fire and metal-working, associated with volcanic fires; from Cretan, *Welkhanoc* (?)

• Enhances magic and provides protection; hence altars and temples were often constructed from lava

VOLCANO

Heat beneath beat beneath convulsive heat/
beat/retreat of fire thrum/drum/sun-hot center polar/pillar penetrates sensate
liquid ore/core heat beneath below

                                               man-
tled bone-fire/stone-fire/bonfire of vagar-
ies "'*ante Vulcunum*,' before fire, art-
ifice, and the yoke of labor"[3] knee-arc
finger-curl shoulder-roil above new-heart-

beat RISE face flesh furnace/blasted new RISE
eye-flame throat-flame neck-flame RISE beyond fire
already pooling golding gilding mass
in open space in CONDENSATION

                                             cool-air
savors heat assuages beat transmuted gold
weds leaden-darkness-crusted-Earth-moist mold

---

[3] Raphael Falco, *Conceived Presences.* Amherst MA: University of Massachusetts Press, 1994) 148; citing Erwin Panofsky.

— W/X —

WAVELLITE

- ❖ Occasionally mined for phosphorous
- ❖ In itself is colorless unless tinted by impurities, resulting in green, blue, brown, grey, white, and yellow
- ❖ Valued as collectors' specimens for the distinctive crystal form

- ➢ *Wavellite*: named after William *Wavell*, its discoverer + *ite* 'mineral or rock', even though cross-sections of specimens often resemble breaking waves

- • Crystals strengthen and heal bones, a consequence of its phosphorus content

WITHERITE

- ❖ Barium mineral, particularly sought after by collectors since it always forms twin crystals
- ❖ Occasionally three twin crystals form joined in a circle, creating a *trilling*
- ❖ Popular as a collectors' specimen

- ➢ *Witherite*: Named after William *Withering*, its discoverer + *ite* 'mineral or rock

- • Crystals ameliorate compulsive behavior, breaking the cycle of negativity

WULFENITE

- ❖ Mined as a molybdenum ore
- ❖ Yellow crystals frequently called 'yellow lead ore'
- ❖ Also used as collectors' specimens

- ➢ *Wulfenite*: Named after Francis Xavier von *Wülfen*, its discoverer + *ite* 'mineral or rock

- Encourages connection to the spirits of nature

XANTHITE [SEE VESUVIANITE]

— Y —

YAG [YTTRIUM ALUMINUM GARNET]

❖ Synthetic GARNET used as a gemstone and in solid-state lasers
❖ Formerly popular as a DIAMOND and other gemstone simulant
❖ Varietal and trade names include: *Diamonair, Diamonique, Diamonite, Diamont, Kimberly, Linde simulated diamond, Yttrium garnet*
❖ Largely supplanted by the introduction of CUBIC ZIRCONIA

YOUNGITE

❖ Agatized breccia, used primarily as cabochons for jewelry and as collectors' specimens
❖ Brecciated (broken, angular fragments of older rock fused into a younger matrix) JASPER, often surrounded by druzy QUARTZ
❖ Frequently described as looking like a "fuzzy brain"
❖ The single source, near Hartville, Wyoming, essentially exhausted

• Facilitates solving difficult problems, particularly when the solution requires physical action

— Z —

ZEBRA MARBLE
- ❖ Striking white-and black patterned marble, used as cabochons or polished free-forms in jewelry
- ❖ Particularly fine zebra marble found in central and southern Utah

- ➤ Named for its resemblance to zebra striping

- • Works against prejudice or xenophobia

ZEOLITE
- ❖ General name for a group of 48 naturally occurring and over 1,500 synthetic types
- ❖ Some 4,000,000 tons of natural zeolite mined annually; over half of that used in China to make concrete
- ❖ When heated, release their water of crystallization; the resulting void may be filled by more water or other materials
- ❖ Used in water purification, water softening, and in aquarium filters
- ❖ Synthetic zeolites used in manufacturing laundry detergent
- ❖ Generally valuable to collectors as crystal clusters; often sold as "Zeolite," without any attempt to identify specific type

- ➤ *Zeolite*: Greek, *zein* 'to boil' + *ite* 'mineral or rock', hence, 'rock that boils'

ZINCITE
- ❖ Rarely forms crystals, except in specimens found near Franklin, New Jersey
- ❖ Many specimens are synthetically created
- ❖ Originally a major source of zinc; important in manufacturing crystal radio before the development of vacuum tubes

- ❖ Primarily important now as collectors' specimens

- ➢ *Zincite*: *Zinc* + *ite* 'rock'

ZINNWALDITE

- ❖ Member of the MICA group, containing iron and lithium
- ❖ Associated with tin

- ➢ *Zinnwaldite*: Named after *Zinnwald*, a village on the border between Germany and the Czech Republic, where it was first discovered + *-ite* 'rock'
- ➢ *Zinnwald*: *Zinn* 'tin' + *wald* 'forest'

- • Encourages dominant genes in children, thereby diminishing the possibility of recessive-gene-linked diseases such as hemophilia

ZIRCON

- ❖ Among the oldest of minerals; specimens from Western Australia have been dated at 4.4 billions years
- ❖ Earliest sources: Greece, 6th Century A.D.
- ❖ Associated with Fire and Water; Mars and Aries; Saturn and Capricorn
- ❖ Traditional birthstone for December
- ❖ First appeared as a blue gemstone (brown stones treated by heat turn blue) in 1920, and subsequently accepted by gemologists as a legitimate gem
- ❖ Most valuable specimens are colorless
- ❖ Also blue, brown, green, red, yellow

- ➢ *Zircon*: Persian, *zar*, 'color' + *gun*, 'gold', referring to color and brilliance; alternatively, Arabic, *zargu,* 'vermilion'
- ➢ *Hyacinth Zircon*: Yellow zircon
- ➢ *Jargon Zircon*: Straw-colored to nearly colorless variety
- ➢ *Starlight Zircon*: Blue variety created by heating other varieties

- • Hindus: Zircon is one of the gems forming the Kalpa Tree of the Hindu Religion—green zircons constitutes leaves
- • 11th Century: Zircon amulets protect travelers from injury and illness; invite hospitality and cordiality everywhere

- 16th Century Europe: Enhances its owner's business sense and perspicacity; a guaranteed ward against being struck by lightning
- 17th Century: Considered a talisman against the Plague

ZIRCONIA, CUBIC [SEE CUBIC ZIRCONIA]

ZOISITE, ANYOLITE, ROZALINE, RUBY ZOISITE, TANZANITE, THULITE

- ❖ *Zoisite*: Confirmed as a separate mineral in 1805
- ❖ *Tanzanite*: A modern gemstone, first discovered in 1966
- ❖ Pure zoisite colorless
- ❖ Varieties of zoisite are named—and valued—primarily by color
- ❖ Ancient to Modern: Artists sculpt figures from anyolite, working from the native shape of the included RUBY crystals
- ❖ Included zoisite occasionally cut *en cabochon*

- ➢ *Zoisite:* Named for Baron Sigmund *Zois* van Edelstein, + *ite* 'mineral or rock'
- ➢ *Anyolite:* Named from Masai, *anyoli* 'green' + *-ite* 'rock or mineral'; green zoisite with black hornblende inclusions and blebs of opaque RUBY
- ➢ *Ruby Zoisite*: Vivid green background, frequently with amorphous inclusions of black hornblende and vivid red or black CORUNDUM, hence, 'Ruby Zoisite'; also occasionally as brown crystals; found in Tanzania
- ➢ *Saualpite*: Original name for zoisite, named for the *Sau-Alp* Mountain where it was discovered + *ite* 'rock or mineral'
- ➢ *Tanzanite*: Named for Tanzania, the only location to date for the deep blue gemstone variant of zoisite
- ➢ *Thulite*: Named for Thule, the ancient designation for Norway, after the initial discovery site of the pink gemstone variant at Telemark, Norway; first discovered in 1820

- Associated with Mars/Ares
- *Anyolite*: Associated with Fire

- Efficacious for heart, lungs, spleen, pancreas
- Transforms negative energies into positive
- Dispels laziness
- Balances those who serve others

RUBY-ZOISITE

Gaudy shimmering
In purple and green—hand-carved
Ruby-Zoisite

SOURCES AND RESOURCES

Butler, Gail A. *The Rockhound's Guide to California.* Consulting Editor, W.R.C. Shedenhelm. Helena MT: Falcon Press, 1995.

Chesterman, Charles W. *National Audubon Society Field Guide to North American Rocks and Minerals.* 25 May 1978. 16th Printing. New York: Chanticleer Press/ Knopf, 1998.

Chocron, Daya Sarai. *Healing with Crystals and Gemstones.* York Beach ME: Samuel Weiser, 1986.

Cunningham, Scott. *Crystal, Gem & Metal Magic.* St. Paul MN: Llewellyn, 1991.

Darling, Peter. *Crystals.* Edison NJ: Chartwell, 1998.

Desautels, Paul E. *Rocks & Minerals.* New York: Grosset & Dunlap/Ridge Press, 1974.

Desautels, Paul E. *The Mineral Kingdom.* New York: Madison Square Press, 1968.

Dietrich, R. V. *Gemrocks: Ornamental & Curio Stones.* Online at: http://www.cst.cmich.edu/users/dietr1rv/Default.htm

Elsbeth, Marguerite. *Crystal Medicine.* St. Paul MN: Llewellyn, 1997.

Evans, Joan. *Magical Jewels of the Middle Ages and the Renaissance.* Oxford, England: Clarendon Press, 1922. Reprint: New York: Dover, 1977.

Fire Mountain Gems. *Jewelry Maker's Catalog*—Year 2000. Fire Mountain Gems: Cave Junction OR, 1999.

Hall, Cally. *Gems & Precious Stones.* Edison NJ: Chartwell Books, 1993, rpt. 1998.

Holden, Martin. *The Encyclopedia of Gemstones and Minerals.* Friedman Group, 1991.

Korbel, Peter, and Milan Novak. *Minerals Encyclopedia.* Lisse, The Netherlands: Rebo, 1999.

Kunz, George F. *The Curious Lore of Precious Stones.* 1913. New York: Halcyon House, 1938. Rpt: New York: Dover, 1971

Kunz, George F. *The Magic of Jewels and Charms.* Philadelphia PA: Lippincott. 1915.

LeGrand, Jacques. *Diamonds: Myth, Magic, and Reality.* New York: Crown, 1980.

Melody. *Love is in the Earth: A Kaleidoscope of Crystals.* Wheat-ridge CO: Earth-Love, 1991.

Pellant, Chris. *Rocks and Minerals.* London: DK Publishing, 1992.

Pough, Frederick H. *A Field Guide to Rocks and Minerals.* 4th ed. Boston MA: Houghton Mifflin, 1976.

Russell, Henry. *Encyclopedia of Rocks, Minerals, and Gemstones.* San Diego CA: Thunder Bay Press, 2001.

Schumann, Walter. *Gemstones of the World.* Revised and expanded edition. New York: Sterling, 1997.

Sofianides, Anna S., and George E. Harlow. *Gems & Crystals from the American Museum of Natural History.* Photographs by Erica and Harold Van Pelt. New York: Simon and Schuster, 1990.

Symes, R. F., and R. R. Harding. *Crystal & Gem.* New York: Knopf, Eyewitness Books, 1991.

Whispering Woods Crystal Grimoire. Online at: http://www.whisperingwood.homestead.com/CrystalSection.html

Yates, Frances A. *Giordano Bruno and the Hermetic Tradition.* Chicago and London: University of Chicago Press, 1964.

ABOUT THE AUTHOR

MICHAEL R. COLLINGS is an Emeritus Professor of English at Seaver College, Pepperdine University, where he directed the Creative Writing Program for over two decades. He has published multiple volumes of poetry, novels, short fiction, and scholarly studies of such contemporary writers as Stephen King, Dean R. Koontz, and Orson Scott Card. He is now retired and lives in his native state of Idaho.